Maimonides on Judaism
and the Jewish People

SUNY Series in Jewish Philosophy

Kenneth Seeskin, Editor

Maimonides on Judaism and the Jewish People

Menachem Kellner

State University of New York Press

Published by
State University of New York Press, Albany

© 1991 State University of New York

All rights reserved

Printed in the United States of America

For information, address State University of New York
Press, State University Plaza, Albany, N.Y., 12246

Production by Diane Ganeles
Marketing by Dana E. Yanulavich

Library of Congress Cataloging-in-Publication Data

Kellner, Menachem Marc, 1946–
    Maimonides on Judaism and the Jewish people / Menachem Kellner.
        p.   cm. — (SUNY series in Jewish philosophy)
    Includes bibliographical references and index.
    ISBN 0-7914-0691-1 (alk. paper). — ISBN 0-7914-0692-X (pbk. :
alk. paper)
    1. Maimonides, Moses, 1135–1204.   2. Philosophy, Jewish.
3. Philosophy, Medieval.   I. Title.   II. Series.
B759.M34K44   1991
296.1′72—dc20   90-44128
                                                            CIP

10 9 8 7 6 5 4 3 2 1

In Memoriam
Steven S. Schwarzschild
1924–1989
Teacher, Friend, Guide

Contents

Abbreviations

HUCA   *Hebrew Union College Annual*

JAAR   *Journal of the American Academy of Religion*

JAOS   *Journal of the American Oriental Society*

JQR   *Jewish Quarterly Review*

PAAJR   *Proceedings of the American Academy for Jewish Research*

REJ   *Révue des études juives*

Preface

Some time ago I published an essay in which I set forth my understanding of Maimonides's vision of the messianic future, according to which, the distinction between Jew and Gentile will disappear by the time the messianic era reaches full maturity. I gave a copy of the essay to my learned neighbor, Mr. Asher Waggenberg. After reading the essay Mr. Waggenberg told me that although he did not contest any of the things I had to say, he still could not bring himself to believe that the position I imputed to Maimonides could really be his. I told him that in his honor I would write an essay in which I explained why the Rambam had to adopt the position I ascribed to him. This study is the result of that promise.

In this book, as in my earlier *Maimonides on Human Perfection*, I seek to present and analyze fairly and disinterestedly, certain themes in Maimonides's writings; I also seek to present and defend a particular interpretation of Maimonides. It was my intention to keep the two sufficiently separate so that even those who remain unconvinced by my interpretation can benefit from the exposition and analysis here presented; I hope that I have succeeded.

I have transliterated Hebrew and Arabic terms without diacritical marks; I did this not only because it was technically much simpler, but because those familiar with the languages do not need them, and those not familiar with the languages are not helped by them. Translations are my own unless otherwise stated.

I am grateful for the assistance of a number of friends who read and commented in detail on this book in the various stages of its development. These include Daniel J. Lasker, Yizhak Gross, Michael Schwartz, Seth Ward, and Rabbi Yisroel Miller; the usual disclaimer about my sole responsibility for what is said here must be emphatically added.

My children, Avinoam David Kellner and Rivka Temima Kellner, were most gracious about allowing me to use my computer from time to time to write this book and for that I am grateful. More than that, I am grateful to them and to my wife, Jolene, for being what they are.

This book is dedicated to the memory of Steven S. Schwarzschild, who, before his sudden death in December of 1989 had read and commented on the first draft. Steven had been my teacher and became my friend. But he was more than teacher and friend, although I certainly valued him as such. To the extent that I have been able to stay honest with myself and the world, it is because Steven kept me honest. He is sorely missed.

1

Introduction

That Jews are distinct from Gentiles is an axiom of Jewish faith and a lesson of Jewish history. But what is the basis of that distinction? Jacob Katz has pointed out that the distinction has been explained in two very different ways. One approach grounds it in theological terms and sees it as "a mere divergence in articles of creed."[1] Katz contrasts this to what we may call an essentialist view, one that traces "religious and historical differences to the dissimilar character of Jew and non–Jew respectively." On this view, "a qualitative difference was involved for which the individual was not responsible and which he could not change." There was, in other words, an *essential* difference between Jews and Gentiles. Katz finds the origin of this view in Midrash, sees its development in Halevi, and attributes its widespread acceptance among late medieval Jews to the impact of the *Zohar*.[2]

There is no doubt that the essentialist interpretation of Jewish identity—*what*, not *who*, is a Jew—finds expression in Midrash and *Zohar* and that it is a central motif in the philosophy of Judah Halevi; it is perhaps less often noticed that discussions that reflect this position in postrabbinic literature are also often informed by a debate between Plato and Aristotle on the nature of the soul.

On Plato's view, we receive our souls "off the shelf," as it were. Just as the soul survives its period of collaboration with

1

the body, so it exists independently before that period. Indeed, everything we are ever truly to know we knew in this preexistent state, and all learning is nothing in the final analysis but a process of recollection.[3]

For Aristotle, the soul is the form of the body. The soul (*psyche*), that is, is the animative principle whereby a human being is a human being. It is the soul that actualizes the potential given us by nature to be human beings.[4] But for Aristotle, form does not exist independently of the matter it actualizes. There can be no talk, then, of preexistent souls "zapped" into the body at the moment of conception or birth. But if the soul does not preexist the body, can it, or some part of it, survive the death of the body? In Hellenistic and medieval times a theory was developed, elaborating on some ambiguous comments of Aristotle's, which accounted for the possibility that some humans, at least, would achieve immortality. For our purposes, the most important aspect of the Aristotelian theory, especially as it was developed by Aristotle's later interpreters, is that our rational capabilities are not given us fully formed. That part, element, or aspect of our souls that most truly distinguishes us from other living beings, that element through which human beings are truly human,[5] exists in us only as a capability when we are born.

Judah Halevi summarized some of the main features of this theory (one that he may or may not have accepted himself; he is not clear on the subject) in the following terms:

> Every individual on earth has his completing causes; consequently an individual with perfect causes becomes perfect, and another with imperfect causes remains imperfect . . . the philosopher, however, who is equipped with the highest capacity, receives through it the advantages of disposition, intelligence and active power, so that he wants nothing to make him perfect. Now these perfections exist, but *in potentia*, and require instruction and training to become practical, and in order that this capacity, with all its completeness or deficiencies and endless grades, may become visible.[6]

On this view human beings are born, *contra* Plato, without innate knowledge but with a capacity or potential to learn.

This capacity is called, depending on the specific version of the theory that one encounters, "hylic intellect," "material intellect," or "potential intellect." If one takes advantage of one's capacity to learn (a process in which God or the Active Intellect play a crucial role), and actualizes one's potential for study, then one will have acquired what Maimonides came to call "an intellect *in actu*,"[7] more often called the "acquired intellect." The question of how one must perfect one's intellect in order to acquire an intellect *in actu*, that is, the question of what one must master, was a matter of debate. In the version of the theory often ascribed to Maimonides, one perfected one's intellect only through the apprehension of metaphysical truths. In the version of the theory adopted by Gersonides, the achievement of true knowledge in any discipline was sufficient to give one at least a measure of intellectual perfection.[8] To the extent that immortality is affirmed, it is the acquired intellect that is seen as immortal. Since one can actualize one's potential intellect to different degrees, it follows that one's perfection, and thus one's share of immortality, depends on the degree to which one has perfected himself or herself intellectually.[9]

For our purposes the crucial elements in this theory are the claims that (a) no human being is born with a fully developed soul—we are, rather, born with the *potential* to *acquire* what can be called a soul; and (b) the only way one can possibly actualize his or her potential to acquire a "soul" is through intellectual activity. On the one hand, this theory commits one to an extremely parochial position: only the intellectually gifted and energetic can ever really fulfill themselves as human beings. This form of intellectual elitism leaves most of the human race out in the cold.[10] On the other hand, the theory also forces one to adopt a very non-parochial stance: anyone born with a measure of intelligence and a willingness to apply oneself to the exacting demands of intellectual labor can achieve some measure or other of perfection. Race, creed, sex, or national origin are simply not issues.

Turning to parallel developments in Jewish thought, we find that Sa'adia Gaon rejected this approach and adopted a modified version of the Platonic theory.[11] Where the soul for

Plato preexists the body, for Sa'adia it is created by God "simultaneously with the completion of the bodily form of the human being."[12] But for both Plato and Sa'adia, the normal human being starts life with a fully formed soul.

There are many passages in rabbinic literature that reflect a position similar to that of Plato's.[13] There are even parallels to his doctrine of recollection. Every Jewish schoolchild knows the *aggadah* to the effect that before we are born we are taught the entire Torah; at the moment of birth an angel slaps us on the face and causes us to forget all that we knew.[14]

Judah Halevi presents no clear view on the nature of the human soul. He twice cites what appears to be the Avicennian reading of Aristotle in the *Kuzari* but it is difficult to judge whether he cites the view and adopts it, or simply cites it as the prevailing philosophical view.[15] What is clear beyond all possible doubt is that Halevi adopts an essentialist interpretation of the nature of the Jewish people, insisting that they are distinct from and superior to all other peoples, and that this distinction is caused by a special characteristic, unique to the Jews, literally passed on from generation to generation.[16]

The *Zohar* is an important expression of the view that human beings are born with fully formed souls. Gershom Scholem summarizes the outlook of the *Zohar* in the following terms: "Like all Kabbalists he [the author of the *Zohar*] teaches the pre–existence of all souls since the beginning of creation. Indeed, he goes so far as to assert that the pre–existent souls were already pre–formed in their full individuality while they were still hidden in the womb of eternity."[17]

We have adduced evidence to the effect that rabbinic texts, Sa'adia Gaon, and the *Zohar* share in common a view that found its classic philosophical expression in Plato, according to which human beings come "factory equipped" with fully formed souls. What is the importance of this? The Platonic view[18] allows one to adopt the essentialist understanding of the nature of the Jewish people. Since God creates souls, he can choose to create them in different ways. This is precisely the express position of the *Zohar*. Jews are differentiated from Gentiles by the fact that Jewish souls are different from (and superior to) Gentile souls.[19] Halevi, without expressly adopting a Platonic view of the nature of the human soul, emphatically adopts an essentialist understanding of the nature of the Jewish people.

If the Aristotelian position commits one to a measure of universalism, then this position commits one to a measure of particularism. Jews are distinct from Gentiles and that distinction is based on a metaphysical difference between them. There is nothing that can be done to overcome that difference. Such a position immediately runs into problems over the issues of conversion to Judaism and prophetic visions of the time when *My house shall be called a house of prayer for all nations* (Isa. 56:7). If Jews are essentially distinct from Gentiles, and if that distinction is grounded in an ineradicable difference in the very nature of Jewish as opposed to Gentile souls, or in some special characteristic that inheres only in Jews, how could one possibly convert to Judaism? No matter how profound one's religious experience, no matter how sincere one's attachment to the Torah and the Jewish people, the hard fact remains that one possesses a Gentile and not a Jewish soul. Similarly, no matter how many swords are beaten into plowshares in the days of the Messiah, the Jews will still have Jewish souls and the Gentiles, Gentile (and thus inferior) souls.

Halevi meets the problem of conversion by arguing that converts are indeed not the equals of native Jews and that only after many generations, so it would seem, can their descendants be fully amalgamated into the Jewish people.[20] To adopt a brilliant and amusing metaphor of Daniel J. Lasker's, just as IBM PC clones may run the same software as original IBM hardware, but are still not the "real thing"; so, too, converts may believe what native Jews believe, and act as they do (software), they are still not the same as native Jews (hardware).[21]

The *Zohar* meets the problem of conversion in two ways. One is to affirm that the proselyte never becomes the equal of the Jew.[22] Alternatively, souls of true converts are souls of Jewish origin and were at Sinai with all other Jewish souls.[23]

That these souls ended up in the bodies of Gentiles is, apparently, the result of some sort of cosmic foul–up. It is, then, their intrinsically and essentially Jewish nature that motivates these individuals to convert to Judaism.[24]

The problem posed by the universalist picture of the messianic era is easier to solve. Jewish particularists from some rabbis quoted in the Midrash through Sa'adia, Nahmanides, *Zohar*, etc., have found no problem in reading the prophets in a particularist, parochial fashion. As Maimonides commented (in another connection), "The gates of figurative interpretation are not closed."

In what follows I want to examine the position of Maimonides with respect to the cluster of issues introduced here. I will show that Maimonides adopts an Aristotelian as opposed to Platonic conception of the nature of the human soul. This philosophical position commits him to a variety of unpopular Jewish positions: he plays down the special character of the Jewish people, and affirms that the difference between Jew and Gentile is theological and not essential (i.e., the difference resides in the "software," not in the "hardware," and is thus, in principle, subject to "conversion"); denies that Jews alone benefit from special divine providence, prophesy, or reach ultimate human perfection; extends an unusually welcoming hand to proselytes; literally defines "who is a Jew" in terms first and foremost of intellectual commitment as opposed to national or racial affiliation, and affirms that in the end of days the distinction between Jew and Gentile will disappear.

In showing the interdependence of philosophical, *halakhic,* and theological issues in Maimonides I will be arguing on a number of fronts simultaneously. I take issue with those who, like Shlomo Pines, want to divorce Maimonides's philosophical concerns from his *halakhic* ones, demoting the latter to the status of an "avocation."[25] Pines interprets Maimonides such that his "legal writings subserve an exclusively practical end and, accordingly, contain no indications of Maimonides's theoretical views which, to some extent, can be gathered—with great difficulty—from *The Guide of the Perplexed.*"[26] Pines's reading of Maimonides's "theoretical views" in the *Guide* can be gathered—with some difficulty—from his introduction to *The Guide*. Among the claims that Pines imputes to Maimonides are that Moses might have been more of a philosopher than a prophet, that there might be no "essential difference among monotheistic prophetic religions" (p. xc), and that God is nothing more than "the scientific system of the universe" (p. xcviii).[27]

Were Pines correct in his reading of Maimonides, the latter could have adopted (indeed, according to Pines, did adopt) positions on parochial religious issues at variance with his philosophical views and saved himself a lot of abuse. His life would have been simpler, and nobody any worse off had he adopted standard, particularist positions on ethics, providence, prophecy, immortality, conversion, messianism, the nature of the Torah, and the nature of the Jewish people. That he did not, and adopted positions on religious issues forced upon him by his philosophy indicates the intimate connection he saw between the two.

Just as I reject Pines's demotion of *halakhah* in favor of philosophy, I reject the opposing view that demotes Maimonides's philosophy in favor of his *halakhah*. This view is not popular in academe today, but it is held in circles where Maimonides is very closely studied and both demands and deserves serious refutation. By showing the intimate connection between Maimonides's views on the nature of the soul on the one hand, and his views on the nature of the Jewish people, conversion, messianism, etc., on the other hand, I undermine the case of those who want to read Maimonides on these subjects as if he were a classic representative of insular parochialism. If Maimonides's place is not among the disciples of Al–Farabi, it is not among the Roshei Yeshiva of Eastern Europe either.

2

Psychology

Maimonides never clearly and explicitly expounded any psychological theory in general or any variant of the theory of the acquired intellect in particular. This is because Maimonides never wrote a philosophical work in the simple sense of the term, a book or treatise devoted to the exposition of philosophical problems as they had been expounded to his day or devoted to the solution of those problems.[1] Of *The Guide of the Perplexed*, for example, Maimonides says, "Know that my purpose in this Treatise of mine was not to compose something on natural science, or to make an epitome of notions pertaining to the divine science[2] according to some doctrines, or to demonstrate what has been demonstrated in them." Maimonides continues, explaining that the books "composed on these matters are adequate." He disclaims any pretensions to scientific or philosophical originality and goes on to say, "If, however, they should turn out not to be adequate with regard to some subject, that which I shall say concerning that subject will not be superior to everything else that has been said about it."[3] Thus, with specific reference to one of his discussions of our issue in the *Guide*, Maimonides notes, "This Treatise has been composed only for the benefit of those who have philosophized and have acquired knowledge of what has become clear with reference to the soul and all its faculties."[4] Since the *Guide* was composed for

9

those who were already familiar with accepted psychological theory, therefore, we should not expect to find such a theory expounded in that work, and, indeed, we do not.

While no contemporary scholarly interpreter of Maimonides has expressed doubts about whether or not Maimonides actually adopted some variant of the psychological theory briefly sketched in chapter 1, no attempt has been made to prove that he did, either.[5] This reflects a particular and prevalent scholarly bias, one that sees Maimonides as very much the product of the Muslim philosophical environment.[6] To a great extent I share that bias but I still maintain that an attempt should be made to collect and analyze Maimonides's statements on the human intellect that may or may not substantiate the claim that Maimonides affirmed some variant of the theory of the acquired intellect and, in particular the claims that humans are born with a potential to learn, which they may or may not actualize, and that it is this capability and its actualization in which their humanity lies.[7] I think this way for two reasons. First, there are those who do not share many contemporary scholarly conventions but are nonetheless very close and careful students of Maimonides's writings; they should not *ab initio* be excluded from scholarly discourse. Second, the fact that the community of scholars agrees on something does not make it true.

Maimonides makes reference to the nature of human intellection in the earliest of his major writings, his *Commentary on the Mishnah*. We find the following statement in the first of the "Eight Chapters" with which he prefaces his commentary to *Avot*:

> Know that this single soul, . . . is like matter, and the intellect is its form. If it does not attain its form, the existence of its capacity to receive this form is for nought and is, as it were, futile. This is the meaning of his [Solomon's] statement: *Indeed, without knowledge, a soul is not good* [Prov. 19:2]. He means that the existence of a soul that does not attain its form, but is rather *a soul without knowledge, is not good*.[8]

Maimonides tells us here that vis–á–vis intellect, the soul is like matter, while vis–á–vis matter it is a form; in the former respect, the soul is like matter (and matter, as students of Maimonides know well, exists potentially, not actually, so long as it is not united with form)[9] and the intellect is its form (that which exists *in actu*). If the soul remains in its material stage (i.e., fails to attain the status of "intellect"), then it will have wasted its *capacity* to achieve this level. A soul that remains material, never achieving intellect, which achievement depends upon knowledge, is *not good*. This is a statement of the theory we just summarized: we are born with a capacity to know; to the extent that we actualize that capacity we become intellects *in actu*—we have *acquired* our intellects; if we fail to actualize our intellects, that capacity with which we are born is wasted and nothing survives the death of our bodies.

In the second of the "Eight Chapters" Maimonides states that the "rational virtues" are wisdom and intelligence, the second including "(a) the theoretical intellect. . . . (b) the acquired intellect [*aql mustafad*], but this is not the place for that; and (c) brilliance. . . ."[10] Especially significant here is the fact, noted by Herbert A. Davidson, that this term (i.e., the *acquired intellect*) does not appear in Al–Farabi's *Fusul al–Madani*, the text upon which Maimonides based his discussion. It was sufficiently important in his eyes for Maimonides to have added it on his own authority.[11]

A point similar to the one just adduced from the first of the "Eight Chapters" seems to come across in another text in the *Commentary on the Mishnah*, this from Maimonides's introduction to the tenth chapter of Mishnah *Sanhedrin*, the well–known "Introduction to *Perek Helek*." Commenting on the rabbinic statement, "In the world to come there is no eating, drinking, washing, annointing, or sexual intercourse; but the righteous sit with their crowns on their heads enjoying the radiance of the divine presence" (Berakhot 17a) Maimonides writes, "The intent of the statement, 'their crowns on their heads,' is the existence of the soul through the existence of that which it knows, in that they are the same thing, as the

experts in philosophy have maintained."[12] One achieves immortality, then, through that which one learns, "*as the experts
in philosophy have maintained.*"[13] This sounds very much like
the theory of the acquired intellect, whereby one achieves
immortality thanks to the knowledge one has acquired. Attributing this view to the "experts in philosophy" strengthens
this supposition. Maimonides seems to be indicating his adoption here of a commonly accepted philosophical theory, and
the theory of the acquired intellect would certainly fit that bill.

Turning to Maimonides's next major work, his *Mishneh
Torah,* we find further indications that he had adopted some
variant of the theory of the acquired intellect. In "Laws of
the Foundations of the Torah," IV.9 Maimonides explains
why the soul can survive the death of the body. "This form of
the Soul is not destroyed, as it does not require physical life
for its activities. It knows and apprehends the intelligences
that exist without material substance; it knows the Creator of
all things; and it endures forever."[14] If the last conjunction
in this passage is construed to mean "and therefore" (a construal certainly consistent with the Hebrew) we find Maimonides saying that one's soul endures forever thanks to the
knowledge one has acquired of the Creator. Given the passage quoted from Maimonides's introduction to *Helek,* and
further passages to be considered later, this seems to be the
best construal we can give this text.

Maimonides makes the point very clear in the next text
which makes some reference to our subject. Commenting
again on the passage in Berakhot 17a to which he alluded in
his commentary to *Helek,* he says, "The phrase 'their crowns
on their heads' refers to the knowledge they have acquired,
and *on account of which* they have attained life in the world
to come."[15] Could he be any clearer? One attains life in
the world to come thanks to the knowledge that one has
acquired.

Turning to the *Guide,* we again find references and indications, but, as already noted, no clear–cut exposition of
any psychological theory. In discussing the term *to eat* in
Guide I.30, Maimonides notes that it is applied figuratively to

"knowledge, learning, and, in general, the intellectual apprehensions through which the permanence of the human form endures in the most perfect of states, just as the body endures through food in the finest of its states" (p. 63). Perfection and "permanent endurance" (i.e., immortality), then, are consequences of "intellectual apprehensions."

In his well–known discussion (in *Guide* I.68) of the claim that God is "the intellect, as well as the intellectually cognizing subject, and the intellectually cognized object" (p. 163), Maimonides makes use of many of the elements of the theory of the acquired intellect: "that before a man intellectually cognizes a thing, he is potentially the intellectually cognizing subject" (p. 163), that if an intellect exists *in actu* "it is identical with the apprehension of what has been intellectually cognized" (p. 164), and the identification of the "hylic intellect" with the "potential intellect" (p. 165). Perhaps most suggestive is the text from this chapter that we had occasion to cite. Maimonides explained that he did not refer here to every aspect of his psychological theory, and explain every issue in it, because his book was intended for those "who have philosophized and have acquired knowledge of what has become clear with reference to the soul and all its faculties" (p. 166). Maimonides tells us here that he is working with what we today would call the standard or received theory of psychology of his day; and that can only be some variant of the theory of the acquired intellect.

Perhaps the clearest reference to the theory of the acquired intellect is found in *Guide* I.70. There Maimonides says:

> For the *souls* that remain after death are not the *soul* that comes into being in man at the time he is generated. For that which comes into being at the time a man is generated is merely a faculty consisting in preparedness, whereas the thing that after death is separate from matter is the thing that has become actual and not the *soul* that also comes into being; the latter is identical with the spirit that comes into being. (pp. 173–74)

Maimonides tells us here that the souls that survive death are not identical with the souls with which we are born. The soul with which we are born is merely a capacity. If we make it actual, it will then be transmogrified into an entity separate from (i.e., independent of) matter. We are told here that human beings are born with a capacity or potential to actualize their souls. To the extent that they do so, their souls will survive the deaths of their bodies. In this passage Maimonides does not say *how* we are to actualize our potential for immortality. Combining this text with those already quoted, however, yields a fairly complete picture of the theory of acquired intellect: we are born with a capacity to perfect ourselves intellectually. If we actualize that capacity we acquire intellects *in actu* and thereby achieve a measure of immortality.

In *Guide* I.72 we find further, and clearer, evidence that Maimonides did indeed adopt some variant of the theory of the acquired intellect. First, in explaining why man, alone among all the denizens of the universe is called a "microcosm," Maimonides points out "that this is because of that which is a proprium of man only, namely the rational faculty—I mean the intellect, which is the hylic intellect; something that is not to be found in any of the species of living beings other than man" (p. 190; compare also, p. 192). Here we have Maimonides using, without special introduction or explanation, a term—*hylic intellect*—clearly associated with the theory of the acquired intellect. Second, Maimonides comments, "Know that it behooved us to compare the relation obtaining between God, may He be exalted, and the world to that obtaining between the acquired intellect and man; this intellect is not a faculty in the body but is truly separate from the organic body and overflows towards it" (p. 193). Here we have the acquired intellect specifically referred to. Like the acquired intellect of the general theory, this acquired intellect is not a faculty in the body, and is separate (compare the text cited from I.70) from the body.[16]

In *Guide* II.4, Maimonides, discussing the Active Intellect, says that its "existence is indicated by the facts that our intellects pass from potentiality to actuality" (p. 257). Here, then, we find Maimonides explicitly telling us that we are equipped from the factory, so to speak, with potential intellects, the actualization of which depends, in some fashion or other, on the activity of the Active Intellect.[17] We have here a central element in every theory of the acquired intellect.

Further evidence in support of our thesis may be found towards the end of the *Guide*. In III.27 (p. 511) Maimonides tells us that man's "ultimate perfection is to become rational *in actu.*" This means that we are born with the potential to become actually rational. Becoming so, then, depends to one extent or another on our own efforts. Then, too,

> the fourth kind [of perfection] is the true human perfection: it consists in the acquisition of the rational virtues—I refer to the conception of intelligibles, which teach true views concerning metaphysics. This is in true reality the ultimate end; this is what gives the individual true perfection, a perfection belonging to him alone; and it gives him permanent perdurance; through it man is man. (III.54, p. 635)

It is the conception of intelligibles that perfects human beings as such, grants them immortality, and through which they actualize themselves as human beings.[18]

We have briefly worked our way through a variety of important Maimonidean texts. From them all we learn that Maimonides indeed affirmed that human beings are all born with the same basic potential to perfect themselves intellectually, that is, as human beings. With respect to the "equipment" with which we are born, we are all much the same. What differentiates us is the use to which we put that equipment.

3

Ethics

Maimonides's ethical theory, as adumbrated in his "Eight Chapters" and in his "Laws of Moral Qualities,"[1] is intimately connected to a particular approach to human psychology. Maimonides's adoption of this particular approach affords further evidence that he viewed all human beings (Jews and non–Jews alike) as, *ab initio*, equal, and that what differentiates among human beings is not the equipment with which they are born, but what they do with that equipment.

Maimonides's first statement concerning the nature of moral behavior and its relationship to psychology is found in chapter 14 of his *Art of Logic (Millot ha–Higayon)*.[2]

> Man's governance of himself is the science which enables him to develop good qualities and to free himself from bad qualities, if he has already acquired them. Moral qualities[3] are dispositions[4] which gradually become more and more fixed in the soul until they are formed into a habit by which actions are determined. Philosophers describe moral qualities as either excellent or defective. Praiseworthy moral qualities are called virtues;[5] blameworthy moral qualities are called vices. Actions resulting from praiseworthy qualities are called good; those resulting from blameworthy qualities are called bad.[6]

Two things are distinguished here: good and bad behavior on the one hand, and excellent and defective moral qualities (virtues and vices) on the other hand. Actions in and of themselves are neither good nor evil; if they proceed from excellent moral qualities they are good, and if they proceed from defective moral qualities they are evil. Ethics, then, is less the science of human *behavior* than the science of human *character*. Another point made in this passage is that moral qualities are dispositions that can be "fixed in the soul," that is, strengthened. Dispositions that are strengthened in this fashion become habits and these habits determine our behavior. Maimonides, then, distinguishes here between the soul as a substratum and its moral qualities.

What is the relationship between the soul and its moral qualities, and how can we modify the latter? These questions are taken up in the next text, which Maimonides devotes to ethics, his "Eight Chapters."[7] The first point to be noted concerning this work is that it relates to matters common to all human beings. "Know," Maimonides says, opening the first chapter, "that the soul of man is a single soul."[8] Maimonides's subject matter here is human beings as such, not Jews. Maimonides draws oblique attention to this in his introductory statement to the "Eight Chapters:"

> Know that the things about which we shall speak in these chapters and in what will come in the commentary are not matters invented on my own, nor explanations I have originated. Indeed, they are matters gathered from the discourse of the Sages in the Midrash, the Talmud, and other compositions of theirs, as well as from the discourse of both ancient and modern philosophers, and from the compositions of many men. *Hear the truth from whoever says it.* Sometimes I have taken a complete passage from the text of a famous book. Now there is nothing wrong with that, for I do not attribute to myself what someone who preceded me said. We hereby acknowledge this and shall not indicate that "so and so said" and "so and so said," since it would be useless prolixity. *Moreover [identifying], the name of such an individual might make the passage offensive to someone without experience and make him think that it has an evil inner meaning of*

which he is not aware. Consequently, I saw fit to omit the author's name, since my goal is to be useful to the reader. We shall explain to him the hidden meanings of this tractate.[9]

Here we learn a number of important facts. Maimonides disclaims originality, telling us that he has used rabbinic sources as well as the works of classical and contemporary philosophers. These philosophers wrote about human beings, not about Jews. We are furthermore told that these philosophers are not cited by name so as not to offend and drive off those readers who judge the truth of statements in terms of their authors and not in terms of what they say. It is these very statements—which, if cited in the names of their authors would be rejected by some of Maimonides's Jewish readers—which Maimonides uses to explain the hidden meanings in Tractate Avot! Maimonides, then, is drawing on philosophical works in order to explain a tractate of the Mishnah. From this we learn that for Maimonides the Mishnah teaches esoterically doctrines taught exoterically by the philosophers and that these mishnaic doctrines apply to all human beings.[10] After all, if we can explain these mishnaic doctrines in terms of texts drawn from philosophical works it hardly makes sense to affirm that they do not apply to the people for whom these works were written.

Herbert A. Davidson has subjected the "Eight Chapters" to close analysis and has found the philosophical text to which Maimonides seems to be making reference here, al–Farabi's *Fusul al–Madani.*[11] While there is some debate over the exact extent to which Maimonides drew from Al–Farabi,[12] there is no doubt that he drew heavily from him in the "Eight Chapters."[13] The psychological and ethical ideas of the *Fusul al–Madani* are not specifically Muslim; the psychological and ethical ideas of the "Eight Chapters" are not specifically Jewish.

I already noted that in *Art of Logic* (a text no less about human beings as such than the "Eight Chapters") Maimonides distinguishes the soul as substratum from the moral qualities as what we might call affectations of it. This is precisely the doctrine of "Eight Chapters." We have here, then, compelling evidence that for Maimonides the souls of human beings are at basis the same. Differences between them relate to the qualities added later in life to this basic substratum.

We see this clearly in the fourth chapter, "On the Medical Treatment for the Diseases of the Soul." Maimonides there distinguishes between the soul itself and its dispositions. As in *Art of Logic* it is these dispositions that are good and bad and the criterion by which we judge specific actions. Maimonides goes on to tell us:

> Know that these moral virtues and vices are acquired and firmly established in the soul by frequently repeating the actions pertaining to a particular moral habit over a long period of time and by our becoming accustomed to them. If those actions are good, we shall acquire the virtue; if they are bad, we shall acquire the vice. *Since by nature man does not possess either virtue or vice at the beginning of his life* (as we shall explain in the eighth chapter), he undoubtedly is habituated from childhood to actions in accordance with his family's way of life and that of the people of his town. These actions may be in the mean, excessive or defective— as we have indicated.[14]

Speaking anachronistically, we see here that for Maimonides nurture, not nature, determines human moral character. In and of themselves, human beings all start with the same clean slate. No individual or group of individuals is born with a moral "edge" over anyone else.

As promised, Maimonides returns to this point in the eighth and last chapter of the "Eight Chapters:" "It is not possible for a man to possess virtue or vice by nature, from the beginning of his life, just as it is not possible for a man to possess any of the practical arts by nature."[15] Maimonides makes this claim because without it human freedom and moral responsibility are impossible:

> I have explained this to you so that you will not think that those senseless ravings fabricated by the astrologers are true. They go so far as to claim that an individual's time of

birth determines whether he possesses virtue or vice and that he is necessarily compelled to perform certain actions. You, however, should know *that our Law and Greek philosophy agree* that *all* of man's actions are given over to him—which has been verified by true proofs. There is no compulsion on him nor is there any external cause which makes him incline towards a virtue or a vice, except for his being disposed by temperament so that something is easy or difficult for him—as we have explained. There is no way at all that he is forced or hindered.[16]

Human beings are free; on this the Torah and philosophy agree. In order for them to be free, they cannot be born possessing either virtues or vices, for this would mean that we are no more to be honored and rewarded for our virtues than blamed and punished for our vices. Just as *all* human beings are born with the potential to perfect themselves intellectually, so they are born with the potential to become virtuous or vicious. *Ab initio* they are all born equal.

This very point is emphasized in the opening line of Maimonides's "Laws of Moral Qualities." "Every single human being[17] has many character traits."[18] Maimonides thus begins his only systematic discussion of ethics in his *halakhic* code in a section called "*Laws [hilkhot] of Moral Qualities*" by referring to a truth of human (as opposed to specifically Jewish) nature, a truth applicable to all human beings. In the sequel he develops the same basic ideas found in *Art of Logic* and in "Eight Chapters."[19]

Since we are all born with basically the same moral potential and with the same lack of inborn character traits, these can be adopted and adapted. "How so?" Maimonides asks, answering that

> a man shall habituate himself in these moral qualities[20] until they are firmly established in him. Time after time, he shall perform actions in accordance with the moral qualities that are in the mean. He shall repeat them continually until performing them is easy for him and they are not burdensome and these moral qualities are firmly established in his soul.[21]

But "what is the remedy for those whose souls are sick?" (II.1), that is, those who have become disposed to evil behavior. "Let them go to the wise men," Maimonides answers, characterizing the wise as "physicians of the soul," and these wise men "will cure their disease by means of the moral qualities that they shall teach them, until they make them return to the middle way."[22]

On the view described here teachers of morality, the wise "physicians of the soul" can help us not only to alter our behavior but change our very characters. This is possible because in a very real sense we are what we believe, affirm, and do; when beliefs, affirmations, and behavior are changed, we change, inherently, intrinsically, and essentially, to the extent that that is possible.

All this reflects Maimonides's basic view that in the first instance human beings are essentially alike. What distinguishes them are qualities that are acquired and that can be changed. In the previous chapter we saw that Maimonides's psychology commits him to the view that all human beings are born alike, with a roughly equal potential for improvement and perfection. Here we have seen that that psychology underlies a view of ethics according to which we are again at basis essentially alike. In the following chapters we will see how this view of the nature of human beings influenced Maimonides's approach to a series of more narrowly religious issues.

4

Providence, Prophecy, and Immortality

We have to this point been concerned with showing that Maimonides adopted an Aristotelian psychology that made it impossible for him to follow Halevi (and others) in the claim that Jews are inherently different from and even superior to non–Jews. In the last chapter I showed how this theory found expression in Maimonides's approach to ethics. In the chapters that follow I propose to examine a variety of issues in Maimonides's thought, issues ordinarily conceived of as relating to narrowly religious or even specifically *halakhic* questions, all of which reflect his Aristotelian psychology. The fact that these disparate issues can be better understood if we assume that Maimonides adopted the theories here attributed to him both lends proof to the claim that he indeed adopted those theories and supports the thesis that Maimonides himself saw no radical discontinuity between his philosophical interests and his *halakhic* concerns.

Not only do the texts analyzed in chapter 2 show that Maimonides explicitly affirmed the theory of the acquired intellect, but reading Maimonides as affirming that theory also helps us to understand other passages in the *Guide*. In III.18 Maimonides maintains that providence does not rest on all individuals equally, but "is graded as their human perfection is graded" (p. 475).[1] He goes on:

In accordance with this speculation it follows necessarily that His providence, may He be exalted, that watches over the prophets is very great and proportionate to their degree in prophecy and that His providence that watches over excellent and righteous men is proportionate to their excellence and righteousness. For it is this measure of the overflow of the divine intellect that makes the prophets speak, guides the actions of righteous men, and perfects the knowledge of excellent men with regard to what they know. As for the ignorant and disobedient, their state is despicable proportionately to their lack of this overflow, and they have been relegated to the rank of the individuals of all the other species of animals: *He is like the beasts that speak not* [Ps. 49:13]. For this reason it is a light thing to kill them and has even been enjoined because of its utility.

Why is it a "light thing" to kill the intellectually unperfected? Human beings when they are born, the theory of the acquired intellect tells us, are not yet truly human beings. They are creatures having the outward form of a human being. Only by perfecting himself or herself intellectually, only by acquiring an intellect *in actu,* can an individual truly actualize himself or herself as a human being.[2] Those who fail to do so are not truly human beings in actuality. They are potential humans who have never actualized their humanity. They are thus like the beasts of the field (since it is the actualized intellect that truly distinguishes the human animals from other animals) and it is thus "a light thing to kill them."

Other issues that have bothered traditionalist readers of Maimonides become clear in the light of our discussion here. The first of these relates to the text just discussed. In his discussion of providence Maimonides takes care to distinguish between humans and non–humans.[3] Individual divine providence extends only to humans, and to no other creatures. Within the category of humans distinctions are drawn, but these relate to intellectual perfection, not to national origin. Nowhere does Maimonides restrict God's special providence to Jews.[4]

Maimonides makes this clear in *Guide* III.17. He presents several theories concerning providence and sums them up as follows:

> All the various circumstances of the individuals among the
> *Adamites* are considered by Aristotle as due to pure chance,
> by the Asharite as consequent on [God's] will alone, by the
> Mutazila as consequent on [God's] wisdom, and by us as
> consequent on the individual's deserts, according to his
> actions.[5]

Maimonides frames his discussion in terms of human beings
("Adamites"), not in terms of Jews.

Maimonides makes explicit his claim that providence is
restricted to human beings a bit further on:

> For I for one believe that in this lowly world—I mean that
> which is beneath the sphere of the moon—*divine providence
> watches only over the individuals belonging to the human species*
> and that in this species alone all the circumstances of the
> individuals and the good and evil that befall them are con-
> sequent upon the deserts. . . . But regarding all the other
> animals and, all the more, the plants and other things, my
> opinion is that of Aristotle.[6]

Maimonides immediately makes clear why providence is restricted to human beings (pp. 471–72):

> According to me, as I consider the matter, divine provi-
> dence is consequent upon the divine overflow; and the
> species with which this intellectual overflow is united, so
> that it became endowed with intellect and so that every-
> thing that is disclosed to a being endowed with the intellect
> was disclosed to it is the one accompanied by divine provi-
> dence which appraises all its actions from the point of view
> of reward and punishment.

Since only human beings are blessed with intellect, only human beings can be subject to providence. Providence, as
Maimonides emphasizes (p. 474), "is consequent upon the
intellect and attached to it."

This being the case, according to what sorts of behavior
are we guided, guarded, and rewarded by providence?
Maimonides makes no bones about it. "Accordingly, everyone with whom something of this [intellectual] emanation[7] is

united, will be reached by providence to the extent to which he is reached by the intellect" (p. 474). Human beings enjoy the benefits of divine providence only to the extent that they perfect their intellects.

This point is made even clearer in the following chapter (III.18, pp. 474–5):

> The divine emanation that exists united to the human species, I mean the human intellect, is merely what exists as individual intellects—that is, what has emanated toward Zayd, Khalid, and Bakr.[8] Now if this so, it follows necessarily according to what I have mentioned in the previous chapter that when any human individual has obtained, because of the disposition of his matter and his training, a greater portion of this emanation than others, providence will of necessity watch more carefully over him than others—if, that is to say, providence is, as I have mentioned, consequent upon the intellect. Accordingly divine providence does not watch in an equal manner over all the individuals of the human species, but providence is graded as their human perfection is graded.

Providence extends to all human beings, and only to human beings. Humans benefit from providence to different degrees, the degree of providential protection, guidance, and reward depending not on whether or not the individual in question is a Jew, but on the extent to which he or she has perfected his or her intellect.

Another issue that has bothered traditionalist readers of Maimonides becomes clear. Maimonides does not restrict prophecy to Jews and in one place, *davka* in a popular work, explicitly affirms the possibility that Gentiles can prophesy.[9] The preconditions for prophecy include physiological, moral, psychological, and, crucially, intellectual perfection;[10] being Jewish is nowhere mentioned.[11] Prophecy, keyed as it is to intellectual perfection, cannot be restricted only to Jews since all human beings are born with an equal shot at achieving that perfection. We are all born, equally,[12] with the capability of actualizing our intellectual potential and thereby "acquiring" an intellect.

Maimonides is one of the very few medieval Jewish thinkers to hold this view. Halevi, for example, restricts prophecy to Hebrew–speaking Jews residing in Israel.[13] Abraham ibn Daud also makes being Jewish a prerequisite for prophecy; he seems to allow for the possibility that in exceptional cases Gentiles can prophesy, but in such cases it is because the Gentile prophecy is in the interests of the Jewish people.[14] Hasdai Crescas also restricts prophecy to Jews in *Light of the Lord* III.v.4 (p. 46a). Crescas's student, Joseph Albo, takes the fact of prophecy's being a uniquely Jewish phenomenon as a given and must then explain "why prophecy existed among the people of Israel in the land of Israel and not among other nations in other lands."[15] Isaac Abravanel, criticizing Maimonides's philosophical approach to prophecy, points out that in point of fact "we find prophecy only among the Israelite people."[16]

Let us examine Maimonides's position on this issue in somewhat greater detail. Maimonides opens his discussion of prophecy in the *Mishneh Torah* ("Laws of the Foundations of the Torah," VII.1) with the following assertion: "It is one of the foundations of religion to know that God causes human beings[17] to prophesy." What are preconditions for achieving this state? Maimonides immediately tells us.

> Prophecy only rests on an individual of great wisdom and great virtue whose inclination[18] never overpowers him concerning worldly matters but whose intellect[19] enables him to overpower his inclination always, and the possessor of a broad and well–settled[20] temperament.[21]

Remember, this is an *halakhic* text, aimed at rabbis and their students. Here we are told that it is human beings, not just Jews, who prophesy. We are also given a list of preconditions for prophecy. Being Jewish is not among them; rather, the first listed condition is intellectual perfection (wisdom).

Maimonides's detailed discussion of prophecy in the *Guide*[22] develops but remains faithful to his exposition in the *Mishneh Torah*. Maimonides opens his discussion by citing three opinions concerning prophecy. The second is that of

the philosophers. "It affirms that prophecy is a certain perfection in the nature of man" (II.32, p. 361). Since this is the
opinion of the philosophers it clearly relates to human beings
as such and not to Jews specifically. The third opinion "is the
opinion of our Law and the foundation of our doctrine. It is
identical with the philosophical opinion except in one
thing."[23] That one difference is that according to the Torah
God can withhold prophecy from one otherwise deserving of
it. If the Jewish doctrine is, that one difference aside, *identical*
with the philosophical opinion, then according to the Torah
as interpreted by Maimonides, prophecy must be a generally
human and not specifically Jewish phenomenon.

　　That this is indeed the case becomes clear when we read
Maimonides's definition of the nature of prophecy:

> Know that the true reality and quiddity of prophecy consist
> in its being an emanation emanating from God, may He be
> cherished and honored, through the intermediation of the
> Active Intellect, toward the rational faculty in the first
> place and thereafter toward the imaginative faculty. This is
> the highest degree of man and the ultimate term of perfec-
> tion that can exist for his species; and this state is the ulti-
> mate term of perfection for the imaginative faculty. (II.36,
> p. 369)

Prophecy, then, is an emanation from God, working first on
the rational faculty and then on the imagination. It would
appear to be a perfection open in principle to all human
beings. But Maimonides immediately qualifies this and says,
"This is something that cannot by any means exist in every
man." Is this the first stage of restricting prophecy to Jews?
No. Prophecy is something that cannot exist in every human
being because not only does it demand "perfection in the
speculative sciences and . . . improvement of the moral habits," but it also presupposes "the highest possible degree of
perfection of the imaginative faculty in respect of its original
natural disposition." Since the imaginative faculty is a bodily
faculty, its perfection depends not only on training but also
on the state of the body at its birth. Some individuals are
simply born with more perfect bodies than others. Such indi-

viduals, having fewer factory defects and more original equipment options so to speak, can achieve more than other individuals, less fortunately endowed by nature. This then, and not national origin or religious persuasion, is the sense in which prophecy is not an equal option for all human beings.

Maimonides summarizes the preconditions of prophecy thus: "The perfection of the rational faculty through study, the perfection of the imaginative faculty through natural disposition, and the perfection of moral habit. . . ." (II.36, p. 372). In principle all naturally well–endowed human beings who turn from evil and apply themselves to the perfection of their intellects can achieve prophecy. Being Jewish is simply not a question here.[24] There is nothing inherent or essential about Jews as such (as opposed to Jews as observers of the Torah) which gives them a better shot at becoming prophets than non–Jews.

Human immortality is another issue where Maimonides's position can be best understood in terms of his views on the nature of human nature. The Jewish tradition has placed relatively little emphasis on establishing clear–cut, normative views on eschatological matters. Maimonides himself says that no one is in a position to know the details of eschatological matters before they occur.

> They are not explicitly stated by the prophets. Nor have the Rabbis any tradition with regard to these matters. They are guided soley by what the scriptural texts seem to imply. Hence there is a divergence of opinion on the subject. But be that as it may, neither the exact sequence of these events nor the details thereof constitute religious dogmas.[25]

But, withal, certain ideas may safely be presented as typical of Rabbinic Judaism as it had developed to Maimonides's day. One of these is that, other things being equal, all Jews will achieve immortality. "All Israelites," Mishnah Sanhedrin X.1 asserts, "have a share in the world to come." As much as it was expected that Jews, as a matter of course, would enter the world to come, it was equally expected that few if any Gentiles would. Indeed, the classic discussion of the issue is framed in terms of the question whether *no* Gentiles would enjoy a place in the world to come, or *some* would:

> R. Eliezer says: no gentile has a share in the world to come, as it is said, *The wicked shall return to the nether world, even all the nations that forget God* (Ps. 9:18); "the wicked shall return to the nether world"—these are the wicked of Israel.[26] R. Joshua said to him: If the verse had said, "The wicked shall return to the nether world and all the nations," and stopped there, I should have agreed with you, but as it goes on to say, "that forget God," it means that there *are* righteous among the nations who have a share in the world to come:[27]

R. Joshua's position, which by Maimonides's time had become the accepted doctrine among Jews,[28] allowed for the fact that *some* Gentiles might achieve immortality (*hish'arut ha−nefesh*, the philosophical way of expressing the idea of having a share in the world to come). But even on this position, immortality for Jews (the wicked excepted) was almost a foregone conclusion, while for the Gentiles, only the truly righteous among them could hope for a share in the world to come.[29]

Maimonides's discussions of immortality, in his *halakhic* works as well as in the *Guide*, simply ignore the whole question of Jews and Gentiles. Immortality, like providence and prophecy, depends on intellectual perfection. Jews have the advantage of the Torah, to be sure, making it more likely that they will achieve both moral and intellectual perfection, making them better candidates for achieving immortality than most Gentiles, but that is an advantage that depends solely upon their obedience to the laws of the Torah and their intellectual acquiescence to its teachings. In principle, however, Jews as such, as opposed to human beings who behave morally and perfect their intellects, have no advantage when it comes to immortality.

In a previous chapter we had occasion to take note of Maimonides's comment on the rabbinic statement, "in the world to come there is no eating, drinking, washing, annointing, or sexual intercourse; but the righteous sit with their crowns on their heads enjoying the radiance of the divine presence" (Berakhot 17a). Maimonides explains this as follows: "The intent of the statement, 'their crowns on their heads,' is the existence of the soul through the existence of that which it knows, in that they are the same thing, as the experts in philosophy have maintained."[30] Here we have a clear–cut explanation of a Talmudic statement in explicitly philosophical terms telling us that the soul survives the death of the body thanks to what it *knows*. In terms of the acquisition of knowledge, Jews are not inherently better off than Gentiles.

Much the same point is found in the *Mishneh Torah*. We quoted passages from "Laws of the Foundations of the Torah," IV.9 and "Laws of Repentance," VIII.3[31] the burden of which is that permanent endurance is a function of intellectual perfection. In an apparently unusual place, "Laws of Tefilin," VI.13, Maimonides tells us that "nothing endures forever and ever but knowledge of the Rock of the Universe." We will see in chapter 5 that this vision of human perfection as defined in intellectual terms, and thus open in theory to all humans, undergirds Maimonides's account of the messianic world.

Perfection of the intellect as an absolutely necessary condition for immortality is a theme found often in the *Guide*. The term *to eat*, we are informed in *Guide* I.30 is applied figuratively "to knowledge, learning, and, in general, the intellectual apprehensions through which the permanence of the human form endures in the most perfect of states, just as the body endures through food in the finest of its states" (p. 63). Intellectual apprehensions, then, are the key to immortality. Typical of Maimonides's other statements to this effect is the following from the last chapter of the *Guide*:[32]

> The fourth kind [of perfection] is the true human perfection; it consists in the acquisition of the rational virtues—I refer to the conception of intelligibles, which teach true views concerning metaphysics. This is in true reality the ultimate end; this is what gives the individual true perfection, a perfection belonging to him alone; *and it gives him permanent perdurance*; through it, man is man.[33]

The discussion here relates to humans generally ("through it man is man") and not to Jews specifically. Immortality is a function of intellectual perfection, not of heritage, birth, or belief.[34] This, like Maimonides's cavalier views on the "utility" of putting to death certain individuals, and his non-parochial approach to the questions of providence and prophecy all reflect his commitment to the idea that human beings as such are only truly human when they have perfected their intellects, and that such perfection is open to all normal human beings, Jews and Gentiles alike.

5

The Place of Gentiles in the Messianic Era

Maimonides's views on the place of Gentiles in the messianic era are made possible and necessary by his philosophical psychology. According to Maimonides, as I will show in this chapter, the difference between Jew and Gentile will disappear by the time the messianic era reaches fruition. For my purposes, it is not important whether this comes about because the Gentiles will formally convert to Judaism, as I understand Maimonides to hold, or because the difference between the two will wither away and become irrelevant as other interpreters maintain.

The biblical, rabbinic, and Gaonic texts available to Maimonides presented him with two broad options concerning the place of Gentiles in the world of the Messiah. On one of them, the Gentiles will remain forever distinct from the Jews and inferior to them; on the other, the Gentiles (or those who remain after the messianic wars) will convert to Judaism. Joseph Klausner surveyed the biblical and Tannaitic materials and there is no need to repeat his findings here.[1] Gaonic materials on this subject are less well–known and it will be useful to cite examples.

Sa'adia Gaon (tenth century) adopts the view that the distinction between Jew and Gentile will always remain. In

Beliefs and Opinions VII.6 Sa'adia asserts that those Gentiles who "mend their ways" will escape the dire misfortunes that will rain down on those who remain obdurate in their opposition to the Messiah. There are four classes of Gentiles who accept the overlordship of the Messiah. (a) The most distinguished of them will serve as servants in the homes of the Jews. (b) Others will serve in the cities and villages. (c) Still others will be farmhands, working the land for the Jews. (d) The last group will return to their countries and be submissive to Israel.

Rav Hai Gaon (eleventh century) takes the opposite view. After detailing the bitter wars in which many of the Gentile nations will be destroyed, Rav Hai writes, "the nations which remain will convert, as it said, *For then I will turn to the peoples [a pure language, that they may all call upon the name of the Lord, to serve Him with one consent]* (Zeph. 3:9) and they will say, *Come ye, and let us go up to the mountain of the Lord, to the house of the God of Jacob, and He will teach us of His ways, and we will walk in His paths, for out of Zion shall go forth the Torah, and the word of the Lord from Jerusalem* (Isa. 2:3)."[2]

The view of Rav Hai can be interpreted in one of two fashions: either today's Gentiles will become full converts in the messianic era (*ger zedek*) or partial converts (*ger toshav*) who observe the seven Noahide commandments but do not become full Jews. We have, then, four options: (a) Sa'adia's view that the Gentiles will remain Gentiles and exist in order to serve the Jews; (b) the first interpretation of Rav Hai's view, that the Gentiles of today will become full Jews by the time the messianic era reaches full fruition; (c) the second interpretation of Rav Hai's view, that today's Gentiles will become Noahides; (d) and the view (advanced by Ya'akov Blidstein) that according to Maimonides the distinction between Jew and Gentile will simply disappear during the time of the Messiah—in effect, there will be neither Jews nor Gentiles, only human beings who worship God in concert.

It is against this background that we can turn to Maimonides's discussion of the place of Gentiles in the messianic era. Maimonides's most systematic presentation of his views concerning the messianic era is found in the closing chapters of the *Mishneh Torah*, "Laws of Kings and Their Wars," chapters 11 and 12.[3] Given the nature of most of his sources and the use made of them by his predecessors, contemporaries, and successors, this discussion has what can only be called a distinctly and remarkably universalistic cast.[4] By this I mean that a careful study of Maimonides's statements leads one ineluctably to the conclusion that he foresaw a messianic period in which no distinction between Jew ("Israelite" in Maimonides's terminology) and Gentile would remain. By the time the messianic era had reached fruition all Gentiles would have become Jews.

One of the signs that a putative Messiah is indeed the Messiah is that "he will prepare the whole world to serve the Lord with one accord, as it is written, *For then will I turn to the peoples a pure language, that they may all call upon the name of the Lord to serve Him with one consent* (Zeph. 3:9)."[5] Maimonides says "the *whole* world," including, it would seem, those who were not Jews before the coming of the Messiah. He continues "to serve the Lord with *one accord*"; those who serve the Lord in the messianic era will do so without divisions, with one intention, and together. Maimonides also says that the Gentile nations who in the premessianic dispensation are likened to wolves and leopards will, in the time of the Messiah, "*all* accept the true religion, and will neither plunder nor destroy, and *together* with Israel earn a comfortable living in a legitimate way,[6] as it is written: *And the lion shall eat straw with the ox* (Isa. 11:7)."[7] Maimonides consistently emphasizes that which unites the erstwhile Gentiles of the messianic era with the Jewish people.

Maimonides's language here is important. The peoples of the world will "all accept the true religion." The Hebrew here is *yahzeru*, literally, "will return." This would appear to be a reference to Maimonides's doctrine, as found in "Laws of Idolatry," I.1 that human beings were originally monotheists. In the messianic world, as in the world before its corruption by idolatry and astrology, all human beings will share a pure monotheism. The term *true religion* (*dat ha–emet*) is also suggestive. Maimonides uses the term in five other places in the *Mishneh Torah*.[8] In each of these places, as even a cursory examination of them will show, Maimonides uses the term to mean Judaism. There is no reason to suspect that only here Maimonides uses the term in some other sense, such as the seven Noahide commandments.[9]

Maimonides hints at his position concerning the place of Gentiles in the messianic world (i.e., that there will not be any) in the following words as well: "The sages and prophets did not long for the days of the Messiah that Israel might exercise dominion over the world, or rule over the gentiles,[10] or be exalted by the nations."[11] The sages and prophets did not long for these things, I submit, because in the days of the Messiah there will be no Gentiles to be ruled.[12] Otherwise, we must ask who will in fact rule in the messianic era? Maimonides has already established that the Gentiles will not rule over the Jews, citing the rabbinic dictum (Sanhedrin 91b), "the sole difference between the present and the Messianic days is delivery from servitude to foreign powers."[13] So the Gentiles are not going to rule the Jews and the Jews are not going to rule the Gentiles. Why not? The difference between the two will have disappeared.

Maimonides closes his discussion of the Messiah, and the *Mishneh Torah* as a whole, with the following vision:

> In that era there will be neither famine nor war, neither jealousy nor strife. Blessings will be abundant, comforts within the reach of all. The one preoccupation of the *whole* world will be to know the Lord. Hence Israelites will be very wise, they will know the things that are now concealed and will attain an understanding of their Creator to the utmost human capacity,[14] as it is written: *For the earth shall be full of the knowledge of the Lord, as the waters cover the sea.* (Isa. 11:9)[15]

This passage, the summit and seal of the *Mishneh Torah*, demands careful reading. Famine, war, jealousy, and strife are all outcomes of divisions among human beings. When such divisions disappear, so do they. Blessings will be abundant, and comforts within the reach of all, Maimonides can be understood as saying, not because of some miraculous change in the nature of the world and of human beings, but

because people (not Jews only, but everyone) will be satisfied
with less. The *whole* world, not just the Jews, will be preoccupied with knowing God. Knowing God—to the extent that
such knowledge is possible[16]—as Maimonides explains,[17] is
the peak and pinnacle of metaphysics. It is also the purpose
and goal of human (Maimonides does not say, "Jewish")
life.[18] Metaphysics is the "depth content" of the Torah when
it is properly understood.[19]

The whole world will be preoccupied, then, with the
study of the secrets of the Torah. The "Israelites" who will be
very wise, and who will attain the utmost of *human* as opposed to parochially *Jewish* success, therefore, cannot be the
descendents of today's Jews as opposed to the descendents of
today's Gentiles. Rather, all peoples in the world will be Israelites, since all peoples in the world will be *full of the knowledge of the Lord.*[20]

The reading of Maimonides presented here, according
to which the distinction between Jew and Gentile will disappear in the messianic world,[21] is strongly supported by other
texts from Maimonides's writings. The first is a passage cen-
sored from most printed editions of the *Mishneh Torah.*

> But if he does not meet with full success, or is slain, it is
> obvious that he is not the Messiah promised in the Torah.
> He is to be regarded like all the other wholehearted and
> worthy kings of the House of David who died and whom
> the Holy One, blessed be He, raised up to test the multi-
> tude, as it is written *And some of them that are wise shall stum-
> ble, to refine among them, and to purify, and to make white, even
> to the time of the end; for it is yet for the time appointed* (Dan.
> 11:35). Even of Jesus of Nazareth, who imagined that he
> was the Messiah, and was put to death by the court, Daniel
> had prophesied, as it is written *And the children of the violent
> among thy people shall lift themselves up to establish the vision; but
> they shall stumble* (Dan. 11:14). For has there ever been a
> greater stumbling than this? All the prophets affirmed that
> the Messiah would redeem Israel, save them, gather their
> dispersed, and confirm the commandments. But he [Jesus]
> caused Israel to be destroyed by the sword, their remnant
> to be dispersed and humiliated. He was instrumental in
> changing the Torah and causing the world to err and serve

another beside God. But it is beyond the human mind to
fathom the designs of the Creator; for our ways are not His
ways, neither are our thoughts His thoughts. All these matters relating to Jesus of Nazareth and the Ishmaelite
[Mohammed] who came after him, only served to clear the
way for King Messiah, *to prepare the whole world to worship
God with one accord,* as it is written *For then will I turn to the
peoples a pure language, that they all call upon the name of the
Lord to serve Him with one consent* (Zeph. 3:9). Thus the messianic hope, the Torah, and the commandments have become familiar topics—topics of conversation (among the
inhabitants) of the far isles and many people, uncircum-
cized of heart and flesh. They are discussing these matters
and the commandments of the Torah. Some say, "Those
commandments were true, but have lost their validity and
are no longer binding"; others declare that they had an
esoteric meaning and were not to be taken literally; that the
Messiah has already come and revealed their occult significance. But when the true King Messiah will appear and
succeed, be exalted and lifted up, they will forthwith recant
and realize that they have inherited nothing but lies from
their fathers, that their prophets and forbears led them
astray.[22]

In this remarkable text Maimonides explains that Christianity and Islam have a messianic role.[23] By preparing the
world to accept ideas concerning messianism, the Torah, and
commandments, they help pave the road on which the Messiah must travel. How so? As we have seen, among the tasks
of the Messiah will be "to prepare the world to worship God
with one accord." This will be accomplished through natural
means. "Let no one think that in the days of the Messiah any
of the laws of nature will be set aside, or any innovation be
introduced into creation. The world will follow its normal
course."[24] But to convert the world to pure monotheism
overnight (to say nothing of acceptance of the Torah and it
commandments) would be an "innovation into creation," a
miracle of unprecedent proportions, extending over the face
of the entire world and persisting forever. There is no natural way of weaning idolators from their idolatry and bringing
them to mature and sophisticated acceptance of God and His

worship without a long process of education. This is precisely the role of Christianity and Islam. It is their job to prepare the world to accept faith in God and in His Torah in order to *call upon the name of the Lord to serve Him with one consent* when the true Messiah comes. Since the peoples of the world will have been educated and prepared at that time by Christianity and Islam, "when the true King Messiah will appear and succeed, be exalted and lifted up, they will forthwith recant and realize that they have inherited naught but lies from their fathers, that their prophets and forbears led them astray."

For our purposes this passage not only reaffirms the universalistic thrust of the rest of Maimonides's discussion, by emphasizing that the role of the Messiah is "to prepare the whole world to worship God with one accord," but indicates clearly that in the messianic world all human beings will accept the Torah and commandments (the Messiah cannot come until they are ready for this). But if everyone in the messianic world accepts God, the Torah, and commandments, wherein could the distinction between Jew and Gentile lie?

Furthermore, when the Christians and Muslims realize "that their prophets and forbears have led them astray," then "they will forthwith recant." Of what will they recant? It can be nothing other than their adherence to their false religions and their rejection of Judaism. This is particularly clear with respect to Christianity. Maimonides tells us here that Christianity claims that the commandments were once binding but have since lost their validity.[25] When the Christians realize that they have been led stray and recant, they will once again admit to the valid, binding character of the commandments. In short, they will return to the Jewish fold. Since Maimonides does not formally distinguish here between Christianity and other religions, the implication would appear to be that all religious communities will convert to Judaism.

The second text that supports our reading of Maimonides is also found in the *Mishneh Torah*. It refers to the following passage from Tractate Berakhot 57b:

Our Rabbis taught: one who sees a Merkulis[26] says, "Blessed is He who has shown forbearance to those who transgress His will." [One who sees] a place from which idolatry has been uprooted says, "Blessed is He who uprooted idolatry from our land; as it was uprooted from this place, so may it be uprooted from every Jewish place, and may the hearts of those who worship it be returned to Your worship." Outside of Israel there is no need to say "and may the hearts of those who worship it be returned to Your worship" since the majority are Gentiles. R. Simeon b. Elazar says, "Also outside of Israel one must say this because they [the Gentiles] will [eventually] convert, as it says, *For then will I turn to the peoples a pure language [that they may all call upon the name of the Lord to serve Him with one consent.]* (Zeph. 3:9)

In "Laws of Blessings," X.9 Maimonides writes:

When seeing a place where idols are worshipped, the blessing is said, "Blessed art Thou, O Lord, our God, King of the Universe, Who hast been longsuffering with those who transgress Thy will." When seeing a place from which idolatry has been eradicated, if it is in the Holy Land, the blessing is said, "Who hast uprooted idolatry from our land"; if it is outside the Land of Israel, "Who hast uprooted idolatry from this place." To both blessings, the petition is added "Even as Thou hast uprooted idolatry from this place, so do Thou uproot it from all places and turn the heart of idol worshippers to serve Thee."[27]

Maimonides thus decides the law according to the view of R. Simeon b. Elazar in opposition to the majority opinion. This decision of Maimonides aroused the surprise of other decisors.[28] R. Joseph Karo, in his commentaries on the *Tur* and on the *Mishneh Torah* opines that Maimonides decided the law as he did because he agreed with the reason offered by R. Simeon b. Elazar for his position, "because they [the Gentiles] will [eventually] convert."[29] This explanation seems most reasonable, especially in the light of what we have just seen. We have here, then, further support of our reading of Maimonides, according to which today's Gentiles (or their descendents) will convert to Judaism in the time of the Messiah so that all human beings *will call upon the name of the Lord . . . with one consent.*[30]

A further indication that our reading of Maimonides's views on the status of Gentiles in the messianic era is correct may be found in an interesting parallelism that obtains between the opening and the closing of the *Mishneh Torah.* As Joel Kraemer pointed out,[31] the *Mishneh Torah* opens with a statement concerning the knowledge of God ("It is the foundation of foundations and pillar of the sciences to know that there is a First Existent") and closes with a statement concerning knowledge of God ("Hence Israelites will be very wise, they will know the things that are now concealed and will attain an understanding of their Creator to the utmost capacity of the human mind, as it is written: *For the earth shall be full of the knowledge of the Lord, as the waters cover the sea*").

The first several chapters of the opening section of the *Mishneh Torah,* "Laws of the Foundations of the Torah," appear to be addressed to human beings generally, and not to Jews specifically. Isaac Abravanel found an indication of this in the first line of the work (just quoted) and was troubled by it. "Of what concern is it of ours," he said in his *Rosh Amanah,* chapter 5, "whether or not this foundation [the first of Maimonides's thirteen principles, concerning God's existence] is the pillar of gentile sciences, *which are not of the children of Israel* (1 Kings 9:20)?"[32] In support of Abravanel's reading, note should be taken of the fact that the term *Israel* appears in "Laws of the Foundations of the Torah" for the first time at the end of the fourth chapter (IV.13).[33] The first four chapters of a work dealing with the *halakhot* (laws) of the foundations of the Torah (which laws are [a] to know God, [b] not to entertain the possibility that other gods exist [c] to know God's unity, [d] to love God, and [e] to fear God) deal with matters of physics and metaphysics and are addressed to all humankind.

I suggest that the parallelism between the opening and closing of the *Mishneh Torah* extends beyond the subject matter, the knowledge of God, to the ultimate audience, all humankind. Both texts deal with the same subject matter, the

knowledge of God. The first four chapters are not addressed
to Jews as such, but to all human beings capable of rational
thought. Considerations of parallelism lend support to the
hypothesis that the last chapters, like the first, are addressed
ultimately to all human beings capable of apprehending the
knowledge of God "to the utmost human capacity." If this is
correct than we have further support for my thesis that in
the messianic era, according to Maimonides, all human
beings will ultimately become Jews.

A further argument may be adduced in support of our
position. Gentiles in this present dispensation can win eternal
reward through knowledge of the Lord.[34] Since that knowledge will be the preoccupation of the entire world during the
messianic era, it seems odd to assert that Gentiles will be
distinct from and subordinate to Jews in the messianic world
while they are both earning their places in the world to
come.[35]

It might be objected to all this that the Talmud says
explicitly that converts will not be accepted in the days of the
Messiah. In two places we read,

> Our Rabbis taught: proselytes are not accepted in the days
> of the Messiah, just as proselytes were not accepted either
> in the days of David nor of Solomon.[36]

Maimonides explains this passage as follows:

> Therefore the courts did not accept proselytes during all
> the days of David and Solomon. During the days of David,
> lest they returned[37] out of fear, and in the days of Sol-
> omon, lest they returned because of Israel's sovereignty or
> the great goodness that then reigned in Israel, for every-
> one who returns from idolatry because of any one of the
> vanities of the world is not a true proselyte."[38]

One who converts for any but disinterested motives, therefore, is not a true proselyte. Maimonides, then, quotes part
of the Talmudic text (the part about conversion during the
days of David and Solomon) and simply ignores the other
part (about proselytes not being accepted in the days of the

Messiah). This is, admittedly, an argument *e silentio* but a persuasive one nonetheless. Maimonides, it appears, simply ignored that part of the rabbinic passage that he did not accept.

This interpretation is confirmed by another passage in the *Mishneh Torah*. In discussing the laws of conversion, a text to which we shall have occasion to revert to again, Maimonides states that in the days of the Messiah proselytes will bring the sacrifice which, according to Maimonides, is part of the process of conversion.[39] Such being the case, there can be no doubt that Maimonides does not accept as binding, indeed he contradicts, the rabbinic statement that proselytes will not be accepted in the messianic era.[40]

It might be further objected that the Messiah will gather the people of Israel to the Land of Israel. Maimonides himself opens his discussion in "Laws of Kings" XI with this claim. That being the case, how can I argue that all the inhabitants of the world will become Jews? Are all the inhabitants of the world to be gathered in to the Land of Israel, depopulating the rest of the world and impossibly overcrowding the Land of Israel? This is an obviously absurd position. Two things must be pointed out. First, Maimonides's conception of the messianic era is of a long historical period. The ingathering of the native Jews will occur toward its beginning, the conversion of the Gentiles later on. Second, there is a well–entrenched rabbinic view that the messianic Land of Israel will encompass the whole world.[41] The adoption of such a position solves the problem posed here.

A third objection must be entertained: granting the validity of all that I have put forward here, perhaps Maimonides's claim that the Gentiles will convert to Judaism by the time the messianic era reaches fruition means that today's Gentiles will become Noahides (*ger toshav*), not full converts, and that as such they will worship the God of Israel but fulfill only the 7 Noahide commandments, not the 613 commandments incumbent upon full Jews.

In order to show that this is not Maimonides's position, we must summarize his comments about Noahides.[42] But first it should be noted that the argument presented here against my reading of Maimonides is strengthened by the fact that Maimonides himself says that the *ger toshav* is accepted only during the time that the Jubilee is practiced.[43] The Jubilee year is no longer practiced in this dispensation, but will be reinstituted in the time of the Messiah.[44] Does this mean that the institution of *ger toshav* will be reinstituted in the messianic era, and that when Maimonides speaks (explicitly or implicitly) of conversion of the Gentiles in the messianic era, he refers to the institution of *ger toshav* and not to the institution of full conversion (*ger zedek*)?

Two points must be made. First, given that the Talmud connects the institution of the Jubilee year to that of the *ger toshav*[45] it may be that Maimonides was simply affirming the Talmudic connection between the two institutions and that nothing further should or must be learned from his comment. Second, it is entirely reasonable to assume that Maimonides thought that the messianic conversion of the Gentiles would be a process that occurred in stages and that some or all Gentiles would go through the status of *ger toshav* on their way to the status of full convert, *ger zedek*.

But this question aside, there are substantial reasons why it is very unlikely that Maimonides foresaw a messianic era in which the Gentiles would become only semiconverts (*ger toshav*) and not full converts (*ger zedek*). Put simply, semiconverts are not separate from the Jews but equal to them; their status is in every way inferior and subordinate to that of the Jews. They are separate and *un*equal. But the main thrust of all the Maimonidean texts we have been analyzing here is that in the days of the Messiah all human beings will stand before God equally and jointly.

What is a semiconvert? Maimonides explains that the *ger toshav* (literally: "resident stranger [alien]") is

> an idolator who has undertaken to forsake the worship of idols and to observe the other commandments made obligatory upon the descendents of Noah, but has neither been circumcised nor immersed. He should be accepted and is one of the righteous of the nations of the world. Why is he called "resident" [*toshav*]? Because we are allowed to permit him to reside in our midst in the Land of Israel, as we have explained in "Laws of Idolatry."[46]

Put bluntly, the semiconvert is a tolerated alien, and nothing more. An analysis of some of the specific restrictions that Maimonides imposes on the semiconvert will make this even clearer.

Jews tolerate the presence of the semiconvert in the Land of Israel, but not in all parts of it. Since Jerusalem is the holiest of cities, semiconverts are allowed no place in it.[47] The semiconvert who wishes to worship God in the Temple must do so as a commuter, one not permitted permanent residence in Jerusalem.

Negative commandment 126 in the list of commandments with which Maimonides prefaces the *Mishneh Torah* forbids Jews to share the meat of the Passover sacrifice with the semiconvert.[48] But one of the signs of the messianic era is that today's Gentiles "together with Israel will eat permitted foods in tranquillity."[49] The Passover sacrifice is the central feature of the Passover service; if the descendents of today's Gentiles will be semiconverts in the messianic world, and thus excluded from the central act of worship on Passover, and not allowed a permanent place in Jerusalem, how then can the Messiah be said "to prepare the whole world to worship God together"?[50]

Since the semiconvert is not one's "fellow" a Jew who maliciously murders such a person with premeditation was not in the first instance punishable by a court (although certainly by God!) since he or she did not thereby directly violate Exod. 21:14, the verse that forbids the premeditated murder of fellow–Jews, and the verse upon which the death penalty in such cases depends.[51]

A semiconvert who accidentally kills a Jew is put to death for the offense. A Jew who kills another Jew in such a fashion is exiled to the cities of refuge.[52]

One may take interest on a loan extended to a semiconvert: it is forbidden to loan on interest to "your brother" and the semiconvert is not a brother to the Jew.[53]

In sum, the spirit and detail of Maimonides's description of the messianic era make it impossible for him to have meant that today's Gentiles will be messianic semiconverts, inferior and subordinate to the Jews of that period.

We have here presented a reading of Maimonides's

statements in "Laws of Kings," XI–XII according to which the distinction between Jew and Gentile will disappear at some point in the messianic era. The distinction will disappear either because the Gentiles will formally convert to Judaism or because the distinction will simply lose significance. My own view is that Maimonides expected the Gentiles formally to become proselytes, while Ya'akov Blidstein holds that the distinction will simply lose significance.[54] In support of my reading of Maimonides in "Laws of Kings," XI–XII, I showed how Maimonides decided an *halakhic* question concerning the recitation of certain blessings on the basis of his view that in the messianic world the Gentiles will convert to Judaism and rejected the Talmudic dictum to the effect that proselytes will not be accepted in the world of the Messiah. Arguments on the basis of consistency with other of Maimonides's texts were also adduced.

This position of Maimonides's on the place of Gentiles in the messianic era is one that traditionally minded readers of his writings find so uncongenial that they don't even see it, despite the clarity with which it is expressed. The reason for this may very well be that the *Mishneh Torah* is most often studied in the context of other *halakhic* works, with little or no reference to the *Guide of the Perplexed* and the philosophical tradition of which it is a part. Reading Maimonides the *halakhist* as if he fit without bends, folds, or mutilations into the chain of *halakhic* decisors stretching from the Talmud through the *geonim,* the RIF, the Rambam (not Maimonides!), and on to the *Tur* and the *Shulhan Arukh* can only lead to distortions. These distortions are understandable if not wholly excusable, especially since Maimonides expresses himself with admirable clarity in the *Mishneh Torah.* The same sort of distortion, from another perspective, occurs when the *Guide of the Perplexed* is studied in the context of other Arabic philosophical works, without reference to the *Mishneh Torah* and the *halakhic* tradition of which it is a part.

Assuming that Maimonides, the author of the *Guide of the Perplexed* and Rambam, the author of the *Mishneh Torah,* were the same person,[55] and that while Maimonides may have had esoteric philosophical teachings, he did not have esoteric *halakhic* teachings, and putting together the material amassed and analyzed here, we find that Maimonides's view on the place of Gentiles in the messianic era is both made possible and necessary by his philosophical psychology. Human beings are born capable of achieving human (i.e., intellectual) perfection. Most human beings fail to actualize that potential because of the circumstances in which they mature and develop. In the present dispensation very few people achieve moral perfection. Without such perfection, intellectual perfection is impossible. It is the point of the Torah to bring its adherents to this perfection, through its attention to morals (*mizvot*) and metaphysics. In the days of the Messiah, when all will jointly admit the truth of the Torah, when war, famine, strife, and discord will disappear, when the knowledge of the Lord will cover the earth like the waters cover the sea, all human beings will be able to achieve their full human potential.

6

Proselytes

In our discussion to this point we have established (a)
that Maimonides adopts the theory of the acquired intellect
in one or the other of its variations, according to which all
human beings are born, not with fully developed, "ready–
made" souls, but with the capacity to acquire an intellect *in
actu* and (b) that Maimonides's positions on ethics, prophecy,
providence, and the place of Gentiles in the messianic era
reflect his philosophical psychology and, indeed, are made
necessary by it. In the present chapter I wish to analyze a
further position of Maimonides's, one that both follows from
the positions just sketched out, and that should set to rest any
lingering doubts about the correctness of the analysis here
presented.

As with the case of the place of Gentiles in the world of
the Messiah, biblical, rabbinic, gaonic, and philosophical
texts presented Maimonides with a variety of options concerning attitudes toward proselytes and proselyting. The biblical texts are straightforward: the command to love the proselyte is repeated over and over in the Bible.[1] The situation in
rabbinic texts is more complex, with negative assessments of
proselytes and proselyting joining the overwhelmingly positive biblical approach.[2] The restrained welcome that Halevi
extended to proselytes was already noted.[3]

It is against this background that Maimonides's welcoming attitude toward proselytes must be examined. One of his best–known and most often printed letters is his responsum to Rabbi Obadiah the Proselyte.[4] Rabbi Obadiah had asked, *inter alia*, if he were permitted to pray to "the God of *our* fathers," since he was not a literal descendent of the Patriarchs.[5] Maimonides responded as follows:

> All those who unify the name of the Holy One, blessed be He, as it is written in the Torah, is of the disciples and household of Abraham, our father, and he returned all of them to the right path.[6] As he returned his contemporaries through his statements and teaching, so he returns all those who convert in the future through the testament he commanded to his children and household. Thus, it turns out that Abraham, our father, is the father of those of his descendents who are proper and follow in his ways, and father of his disciples, they being all converts who convert.[7]

According to Maimonides, then, descent from Abraham ceases to be a biological matter and becomes a religious issue. In the terms used above, Maimonides here denies the essentialist interpretation of Jewish identity, affirming that Jewish identity involves theory and practice but nothing more. And he does this specifically in the context of a discussion of *descent*. Jewish identity is, *contra* Halevi, not a matter of genes, but of commitment.[8] Abraham is as much the father of his disciples as he is of Isaac and his progeny. By tracing the proselyte's lineage directly to the Patriarch Abraham, Maimonides puts it on a par with that of native Jews. "In that you have entered under the wings of the Shekhinah and joined God, there is no difference between us and you . . . there is no difference at all between us and you in any matter."[9] Indeed, Maimonides goes even further, maintaining that the *yihus*, lineage, of the proselyte is greater than that of the native Jew. "Let not your lineage be base in your eyes, for if we link our lineage to Abraham, Isaac, and Jacob, you link your lineage to He Who spoke and the world came into being."[10] If the native Jews traces his or her lineage to the Patriarchs, the proselyte traces his or her lineage to God! Maimonides reaffirms this assessment, once again linking the proselyte to God, in another letter he wrote to Rabbi Obadiah:

> Know that the obligation which the Torah has placed upon us with respect to converts is great: with respect to father and mother, we have been commanded with respect to honor and awe, and with respect to prophets, to obey them, and it is possible for one to honor, hold in awe, and obey one whom one does not love; but with respect to converts, we have been commanded concerning love, something which is given over to the heart—*Ye shall love the convert* (Deut. 10:19), as we have been commanded to love His name—*Thou shalt love the Lord your God* (Deut. 6:5) and the Holy One, blessed be He, loves the convert, as it says, *and loveth the convert, in giving him food and raiment.* (Deut. 10:18)[11]

The relationship we are commanded to have with our parents is honor and awe; with the prophet, obedience; but concerning only two beings are we commanded to love: God and the proselyte! Once again, Maimonides emphasizes in the clearest possible terms his warmly positive attitude toward proselytes.[12]

It might be objected, of course, that talk is cheap and that in a private letter to an individual proselyte Maimonides could express himself in a loose, nonobligatory fashion, engage in hyperbole, and give vent to ideas that he would hardly hold in a more sober moment. An examination of Maimonides's comments on conversion and proselytes in his *Mishneh Torah*, however, totally refutes this supposition and confirms in the clearest possible fashion that the ideas expressed by Maimonides in his letters to Rabbi Obadiah reflect his firmly held and *halakhically* based views.

In "Laws of Moral Qualities (*De'ot*)," VI.4 Maimonides points out that the love of proselytes involves the fulfillment of two distinct commandments and that God Himself expresses His love of proselytes. In "Laws of the Sabbath," XX.14 Maimonides baldly (and not quite accurately)[13] states that "a proselyte is like a Jew in every way."

More important for our purposes is Maimonides's treatment of the laws of conversion themselves. In many places the *Mishneh Torah* is little more than a Hebrew translation and reworking of Talmudic texts. Much can be learned concerning Maimonides's views from the way in which he handles his source texts.[14] Divergences from those sources are significant indicators of Maimonides's own positions. One such very suggestive text is "Laws of Forbidden Intercourse," XIII–XIV, where Maimonides codifies the laws of conversion. This text is important for our understanding of Maimonides's conception of the place and nature of dogma in Judaism and I have discussed that aspect of it other places.[15] It is no coincidence, I think, that this text also serves as an important source of information concerning Maimonides's own unusual, if not unique, attitudes toward proselytes.

Maimonides chooses[16] to open his discussion (XIII.1–4) by restating a noteworthy rabbinic source.

> With three things did Israel enter the covenant: circumcision, immersion, and sacrifice. Circumcision was [done] in Egypt . . . and immersion took place in the wilderness, before the giving of the Torah. . . . Sacrifice—as it says, . . . and so it is for all generations, when a Gentile wishes to enter the covenant and shelter under [lit. stand at the threshold of] the wings of the Shekhinah, and accept upon himself the yoke of Torah, he needs circumcision, immersion, and the bringing of a sacrifice . . . and when the Temple will be [re]built, he will bring his sacrifice.[17]

In this remarkable passage Maimonides expresses the outlook that the children of Israel themselves are converts to Judaism. "Native" Jews converted at Sinai in a tripartite ceremony; proselytes today convert in the very same way (or would, were the Temple standing, and will, when it is rebuilt).[18]

In chapter 14 Maimonides basically paraphrases into Hebrew the discussion in Yevamot 47a–b, which forms the basis for all the *halakhot* of conversion.[19] In a few places the paraphrase diverges from its source. One of them is of significance for us. The Talmud says that we are not to belabor nor overdo the discussion of the punishment for sins that will devolve upon the proselyte once his or her conversion is finalized. Maimonides is not content with that, and expatiates at some length. "We neither belabor the point nor enter into details [thus far the Talmudic source]; lest this trouble him and cause him to turn from a good way to a bad way. For at the beginning one only *attracts* a person with soft and pleasing words, and so it says, *I will draw them with cords of a man* and only afterwards *with bands of love* (Hos. 11:4)."[20] Once a potential proselyte had come, the Rabbis sought to disuade him or her (Yevamot 47a; "Forbidden Intercourse," XIV.1); only if such dissuasion failed were we to accept the individual, and then all efforts at dissuasion must cease. Maimonides, it seems, goes further. Once an individual has expressed sincere interest in conversion, it is incumbent upon us to attempt to *attract* him or her to the faith and practice of Judaism.

Maimonides's welcoming attitude toward proselytes find further expression in an influential *halakhic* decision of his. Concerning the recitation made with the bringing of the first fruits (*bikkurim*) the Mishnah (Bikkurim I.4) states unequivocally, "These bring and do not recite: the proselyte brings but does not recite since he cannot say, *which the Lord has sworn to our fathers to give to us*" (Deut. 26:3). Maimonides, apparently basing himself on a source in the Palestinian Talmud (T. J. Bikkurim IV.1), decides the law against the Mishnah (in his commentary *ad loc.*) and even explains his reasoning. He explains that Abraham is also the father of the proselytes [not just of the native Jews] and therefore they, too, can truly speak of the land of Israel as the land *which the Lord has sworn to our fathers to give to us*.[21] Now, it is not unheard–of to decide the law on the basis of the Palestinian Talmud as opposed to the Mishnah where they conflict, but it is not common either. We seem to have another example here of Maimonides's attempts to make proselytes to Judaism feel as welcome as possible.[22]

This overall approach is further reflected in a passage near the end of the *Mishneh Torah*. In "Laws of Kings," VIII.10 Maimonides makes the following observation: "Moses, our teacher, bequeathed the Torah and commandments to Israel only, as it is said, *an inheritance of the congregation of Jacob* (Deut. 33:4) and to all those who wish to convert from among the other nations, as it said *as ye are, so shall the proselyte [be before the Lord]*" (Num. 15:15).[23] "All those who wish to convert" are here, in effect, invited to do so and thus to share in the Torah and commandments. Moreover, the context of this discussion is importantly instructive, and adds urgency to the interpretation of it that I have here given. Maimonides is here discussing the laws of the *yefat to'ar*, the beautiful captive (Deut. 21:10–14). This is, perhaps, the prime example of a person forcibly merged with the Jewish people. It is specifically in this context, with its many harsh prescriptions, that Maimonides sees fit to extend a hand of welcome to "all those who wish to convert."[24]

But perhaps the most notable of Maimonides's statements concerning proselytization occurs in another context altogether. This may account for the fact that while several scholars have taken note of it for one reason or another, none, to the best of my knowledge, have noted its significance for Maimonides's attitude toward converts and conversion. Maimonides was asked whether the statement of R. Johanan (Sanhedrin 59a) to the effect that a Gentile who studies Torah incurs the penalty of death was actual law and that one must, therefore, refrain from teaching Gentiles any of the commandments beyond the seven Noahide commandments.[25] Maimonides answers as follows:

> It is the halakhah without a doubt. When the hand of Israel is uppermost over them, we restrain him from studying Torah until he converts. But he is not to be killed if he studied Torah, since it says, "incurs the penalty of death" [*hayyav mitah*], but does not say, "is put to death" . . . It is permissable to teach the commandments to Christians and attract them to our religion, but none of this is permissable to Muslims.

Maimonides goes on to explain that Muslims reject the authenticity of the Torah and thus cannot be convinced by proof texts brought from it. It appears that Maimonides feels that teaching Muslims the Torah by way of attracting them to

Judaism is a lost cause and thus not to be undertaken.[26] "But the uncircumcised ones," Maimonides continues, referring to the Christians, "believe that the text of the Torah has not changed." They misinterpret it, but do not reject it. By showing them the correct interpretation "it is possible that they will return to the right way."[27]

What is really remarkable about this text is the way in which Maimonides states that Jews may actively proselytize. We are told here that it is permissable to teach the Torah to Christians in order to attract them to Judaism. What stares us in the eyes here is evidence, not only for a positive attitude toward proselytes, but, a positive attitude toward proselytization. It is almost otiose to add that a person who has so positive an approach to the process of proselytization can hardly have a negative attitude toward proselytes, the outcome of the process.[28]

There are a number of texts from the *Mishneh Torah* that might be cited as counterexamples to the thesis defended here concerning Maimonides's attitude toward converts and that should be discussed. In "Laws of Forbidden Intercourse," XV.7 Maimonides says that "an assembly of converts is not called an *assembly of the Lord*" (Deut. 23:3). This seems to be an unnecessary form of discrimination. Why should not a group of proselytes be called "an assembly of the Lord?" A number of points have to be made. First, Maimonides is apparently basing himself on Kiddushin 73a where, for technical reasons, it is stated that a group of proselytes is not to be called "an assembly" (*kahal*). In this passage the Talmud seems to want to make it impossible to separate converts off into a separate assembly (see folios 70a–b), a position that Maimonides would enthusiastically want to endorse. Second, it must be noted that Maimonides uses this claim to ameliorate the lot of the *mamzer* (bastard). The bastard is not allowed to enter the assembly of the Lord (Deut. 23) and therefore may not marry normal Jews; by excluding proselytes from the category of "assembly of the Lord," Maimonides, while in no way harming the converts, dramatically widens the circle of eligible partners for bastards.

Second, Maimonides quotes the well–known passage

from the Talmud, "Proselytes are as hard for Israel [to bear] as scabs."[29] One might have expected Maimonides to have done everything in his power *not* to draw attention to this passage; yet here we find it, blatantly cited in the *Mishneh Torah*, precisely in the midpoint of Maimonides's discussion of conversion. Closer attention to Maimonides's text, however, shows that, far from this being a withdrawal from his overall attitude toward proselytes, it is a confirmation of it. The full text of the passage in Kiddushin goes as follows:

> R. Hamma b. R. Hanina said: "The Holy One, Blessed be He, does not cause His Shekhnah to rest except upon the pedigreed families of Israel. . . ."[30] Rabba bar Rav Huna said: "This is the extra advantage which Israel has over the proselytes. . . ." R. Helbo said, "Proselytes are as hard for Israel [to bear] as scabs."

Once again we see Maimonides expressing his own opinions by judicious editing of talmudic texts. Having edited out two–thirds of the passage, Maimonides then qualifies and explains the rest. "Forbidden Intercourse," XIII.17 talks of individuals who had "slipped through" the conversion procedure inappropriately. They may have converted insincerely, but their conversions are valid. "That is why Samson and Solomon kept their wives," Maimonides concludes, "even though their secret [ulterior motives] were discovered."[31] He then opens the next paragraph by stating, "This is why the Sages said that proselytes are as hard for Israel [to bear] as scabs." It is *insincere* proselytes *only* who are as hard to bear as scabs.

Maimonides's position on converts is dramatically opposed to that of Halevi and to that which would later find expression in the *Zohar* and more overtly positive than that of the other codifiers. Sincere converts are emphatically welcomed and in every way possible made the equal if not the superiors of native Jews. Since becoming a Jew had nothing to do with one's metaphysical essence, but everything to do with one's ideas, and since in the end of days all human beings will ultimately convert, Maimonides had every reason to encourage proper proselytes. It may not even be too far-

fetched to suggest that his propagandizing in favor of converts was part of his messianic behavior.[32]

Maimonides's position on proselytes, just like his position on the ultimate conversion of all Gentiles to Judaism in
the messianic era, is made both possible and necessary by his
acceptance of the theory of the acquired intellect. In terms of
their "hardware" all human beings are alike. They differ on
the level of "software." Software conversions are possible,
both in the world of computers and in the world of human
beings ("liveware"). Sincere acceptance of the teachings of
the Torah is entirely possible and is sufficient (when ratified
by *halakhic* formalities, at least in this dispensation)[33] to make
one a Jew in every respect. Maimonides's philosophical psychology brings him to adopt a perhaps unprecedentedly welcoming attitude toward proselytes.

7

What Is a Jew?

Maimonides's statements on the nature of dogma in Judaism and their relationship to the issue of "who or what is a Jew," raise questions that can best be answered if we recall that Maimonides denies all forms of the essentialist interpretation of the nature of Jewish identity and affirms some variant of the theory of the acquired intellect.

It is well–known that in the introduction to his commentary to the tenth chapter of Mishnah Sanhedrin, Maimonides lays down thirteen roots or foundations that every Jew must hold.[1] Maimonides concludes his statement of these principles with the following peroration:

> When all these foundations are perfectly understood and believed in by a person he enters the community of Israel and one is obligated to love and pity him and to act towards him in all the ways in which the Creator has commanded that one should act towards his brother, with love and fraternity. Even were he to commit every possible transgression, because of lust and because of being overpowered by the evil inclination, he will be punished according to his rebelliousness, but he has a portion [of the world to come]; he is one of the sinners of Israel. But if a man doubts any of these foundations, he leaves the community [of Israel], denies the fundamental, and is called a sectarian, *epikoros*, and one who "cuts among the plantings." One is required to

hate him and destroy him. About such a person it was said,
Do I not hate them, O Lord, who hate thee? (Ps. 139:21)[2]

Maimonides's statement of his principles occurs at the end of
a passage in which he defines the terms appearing in Mishnah Sanhedrin X.1. ("All Israelites have a share in the world
to come".) One term alone remains undefined, *Israelites.* He
appears to have posited his principles here at least in part in
order to define this term. An Israelite is one who affirms the
thirteen principles.[3]

The text here, with which Maimonides closes his statement of the principles of the Torah, turns out, on close examination, to be quite remarkable. In the first instance, we
see that Maimonides defines a Jew in terms of his or her
acceptance of the principles. "When all these foundations are
perfectly understood and believed in by a person he enters
the community of Israel." That Maimonides took this theological answer to the question: "Who is a Jew?" seriously is
evidenced by the fact that he attaches to the acceptance of his
principles the *halakhic* rights that Jews may demand of their
fellows—to be treated with love, pity, and fraternity,[4] and by
the further fact that he here makes one's portion in the
world to come—that is, one's personal salvation—dependent
upon the acceptance of the thirteen principles. Furthermore,
Maimonides makes admittance to the world to come condi-
tional solely on the acceptance of his principles, explicitly
divorcing *halakhic* obedience from the equation ("even were
he to commit every possible transgression. . . .").[5]

Second, if one simply casts doubt upon any of the principles (i.e., does not overtly deny them), one excludes oneself
from the people of Israel. Such an individual must be hated[6]
and destroyed and loses his or her share in the world to
come.[7]

Third, Maimonides makes absolutely no provision for
the possibly of inadvertence playing an exculpatory role
when it comes to doubting or denying principles of faith.
Even if one denies a principle of faith because one thinks
mistakenly that one is following the teaching of the Torah,
one has lost one's share in the world to come.[8]

Further evidence of the seriousness with which Maimonides take his doctrinal definition of "who is a Jew" may be found in the way in which he insists on doctrinal orthodoxy as a prerequisite for being considered a Jew and for earning a share in the world to come throughout his writings. He repeats the thirteen principles with almost no changes in his "Laws of Repentance," III, there also threatening with extinction all who deny any of them. In his "parable of the palace" in *Guide of the Perplexed* III.51 he makes clear that doctrinal error leads to a loss of one's portion in the world to come.

Maimonides emphasizes the seriousness of his characterization of the principles of faith as what may be called dogmas in the strictest sense of the word in his commentary to Mishnah Sanhedrin X.2. The Mishnah states, "Three kings and four commoners have no portion in the world to come." Maimonides explains:

> These are mentioned because of their great degree of wisdom. One might think that because of their great wisdom and by virtue of the Torah of which they know much that they would have a portion [in the world to come]. There [the Mishnah] made it known to us that the foundations of faith were corrupted by them and they had doubts concerning some of them. They were therefore excluded from life in the world to come.[9]

Maimonides continues in the same vein in his commentary to the next mishnah (X.3). "Anyone who destroys one of these foundations which I have explained to you has left the community of Torah adherents."

Maimonides's theological definition of what a Jew is (or theological addendum to the standard definition) had direct *halakhic* consequences. As noted above, there are differences between the Talmudic account of the conversion procedure and Maimonides's version of it, differences for which there is no known rabbinic source.[10] We noted some of the differences that relate to Maimonides's attitude toward proselytes; here I want to draw attention to differences that relate to Maimonides's attitude toward the process of conversion.

I here cite the Talmudic source, putting Maimonides's additions in square brackets.

> Our Rabbis taught: If at the present time a man desires to become a proselyte, he is to be addressed as follows: "What reason do you have for desiring to become a proselyte? Do you not know that Israel at the present time are persecuted and oppressed, despised, harrassed, and overcome by afflictions?" If he replies, "I know and yet am unworthy," he is accepted forthwith. [He should then be made acquainted with the principles of the faith, which are the oneness of God and the prohibition of idolatry. These matters should be discussed in great detail]; and given instruction [though not at great length] in some of the minor and some of the major commandments. . . . He is also told of the punishment for the transgression of the commandments. . . . And as he is informed of the punishment for the transgression of the commandments, so he is informed of the reward granted for their fulfillment.[11]

Through two small additions Maimonides turns the Talmudic passage inside out. Where the emphasis there was entirely on *kabbalat ol mizvot* (acceptance of the yoke of the commandments) Maimonides makes the crux of conversion into a theological matter. The proselyte is instructed in detail on the principles of faith; we are explicitly instructed not to expatiate at length on the commandments.

Just as Maimonides's theological conception of who a Jew is affects his *halakhic* pronouncements, so does his allied conception of who a Jew is not.[12] In many passages in the *Mishneh Torah* and in his *Responsa* Maimonides defines heretics (*minim, kofrim*, and *epikorsim*) in terms of the beliefs they affirm or reject, reads them out of the Jewish community and out of the world to come, and imposes harsh penalties upon them, going so far as to invite vigilantes to kill them outright without benefit of trial.[13]

Given that the standard *halakhic* definition of a Jew is a person born of a Jewish mother or properly converted to Judaism (with no reference in the classic discussions to acceptance of "the principles of faith"), Maimonides's insistence on seeing the issue in theological terms[14] demands an explanation. I have tried to provide such explanations in two previous studies. In one place I offered an explanation in terms of Maimonides's adoption of a propositional ("belief that") as opposed to experiential/dispositional ("belief in") definition of the term *belief*.[15] In another context I offered a second, complementary explanation, reading Maimonides's statements on "who is a Jew" in terms of his universalistic conception of the messianic era as sketched out in chapter 3.[16]

My discussion in this book allows us to reach a broader and deeper understanding of Maimonides and provides us with the tools for understanding Maimonides's theological definition of the nature of Jewish identity. Jacob Katz's distinction, cited at the beginning of this study, is helpful here. He posited that by the end of the Middle Ages "distinctions on theological grounds were superseded by those based on differences in kind and essence—a characteristic trend in contemporary thinking on the role of the Jew in the Gentile world."[17] Maimonides's discussion of "who is a Jew" and his insistence on defining a Jew solely or in large part in dogmatic and theological terms (i.e., in terms of "software") is a reflection of his rejection of all "essentialist" definitions of the nature of Jewish identity. He, indeed, sees the difference in terms of "distinctions on theological grounds."[18] This approach, in turn, is made possible and indeed necessary by his antecedent adoption of a psychological theory according to which *all* human beings are born with a potential to apprehend abstract truths.

We have in this chapter of this study once again shown another aspect of Maimonides's thought that is a direct outcome of his philosophical psychology. Maimonides defines the Jew, first and foremost, in the two places over which he has "control"[19]—conversion to Judaism and access to the world to come (the context of his discussion of dogma, it will be recalled)—, in terms of the acceptance or rejection of certain doctrines. It is nothing "essential" about the person himself or herself that makes him or her a Jew. At basis all human beings are the same. What differentiates them, in religious terms, at least, is the doctrines that they accept or reject. It is on the basis of those doctrines (their "software") that they are accepted as Jews and accepted into the world to come.

8

The Nature of Torah

I have shown here that Maimonides adopted a psychological theory, widely accepted in his day, according to which *all* human beings are born with a potential to apprehend abstract truths. Those who actualize that potential, be they Jew or Gentile, have achieved some measure or other of human perfection. The more of this potential they actualize, the more they will be providentially cared for and the closer they come to prophecy. They will also be approximating what appears to be the messianic definition of the Jew, one who is "full of the knowledge of the Lord." Maimonides's statements about dogma, analyzed here, indicate that at bottom a Jew is defined by the doctrines he or she holds. In this present, premessianic dispensation, where not everyone is yet a Jew, certain *halakhic* formalities must be followed before one's ideological Judaism, so to speak, becomes *halakhic* Judaism.[1]

What is the nature of the abstract truths that must be apprehended, and what is the relationship between that apprehension and the Torah?

Mishnah Hagigah II.1 places restrictions on the number and kind of people to whom one may teach certain matters. "One is not to expound upon forbidden sexual relations in the presence of[2] three, upon *ma'aseh bereshit* in the presence of two, and on the *merkavah* in the presence of one, unless he is wise and understands by himself." The term *ma'aseh bereshit* is usually taken to mean the true meaning of the biblical accounts of creation at the beginning of the book of Genesis, while *ma'aseh merkavah* is understood as referring to the true meaning of the account of the chariot in the first chapter of Ezekiel.

In his commentary on this text Maimonides first explains that the Mishnah brings up this issue here because, having discussed *gufei Torah* in the first chapter of the tractate, it here discusses matters that are "principles[3] of the *gufei Torah*."[4] What are *gufei Torah*? Maimonides adopts the term here, at the beginning of the second chapter of Mishnah Hagigah, because of its appearance at the end of the first chapter (I.8). In "Laws of Idolatry," II.8 Maimonides uses the term to mean the specific, discrete commandments of the Torah. That appears to be the commonly accepted meaning of the term in rabbinic contexts.

What, then, are *ma'aseh bereshit* and *ma'aseh merkavah*, the principles of the *mizvot*, the specific commandments of the Torah? Maimonides says that the Sages call *ma'aseh bereshit* "the natural sciences and research into the beginning of the creation." Their intention in using the term *ma'aseh merkavah*, he says in the commentary on Mishnah Hagigah, is "the divine science,[5] it being speech on existence in general,[6] on the existence of the Creator, His knowledge and attributes, that existent beings necessarily derive their existence from Him, the angels, the soul, the intellect that cleaves to man, and what comes after death." Maimonides explains that these sciences have to be restricted because, "it is known that every man by his nature desires all the sciences, whether he be foolish or wise." This statement is a paraphrase of the well–known opening line of Aristotle's *Metaphysics*: "All men by nature desire to know."

Maimonides's comments here can be better understood in light of a passage from his earliest known work, *Art of Logic* (*Millot ha–Higayon*):

> The term "philosophy" is also a homonym, sometimes signifying demonstration, and sometimes the sciences. In the

latter sense it is given to the two classes of science, one of which is called theoretical philosophy, and the other practical philosophy or human philosophy, or political philosophy. Theoretical philosophy is divided into three parts: mathematics, physics, and the divine science[7]. . . . Divine Science is divided into two parts. One of them is the study of every being which is not matter nor a force in matter, that is to say, whatever appertains to God, may His name be exalted, and, also, according to the opinion of the philosophers, to angels; for they deny that angels are corporeal, and call them transcendent intelligences, i.e., separated from matter.[8]

We are informed here that divine science is part of theoretical philosophy and deals with transcendent ("separate") entities, most notably God and, according to the philosophers, angels. Among the philosophers who include the study of angels in divine science, it turns out, is Maimonides himself. This is not only clear from his discussions in *Guide* II. 2–12, but also from the *Mishneh Torah*. The subject matter of the first two chapters of "Laws of the Foundations of the Torah," the opening section of the *Mishneh Torah,* is *ma'aseh merkavah*.[9] One of the subjects taken up there is the nature of the angels. In the Hagigah commentary we learned that *ma'aseh merkavah* = divine science. In *Art of Logic* we learn that some philosophers include the study of angels in divine science. In "Foundations of the Torah" we see that Maimonides includes the study of the angels in *ma'aseh merkavah*. Maimonides, therefore, is himself one of those philosophers who includes the study of angels in divine science.[10]

In the Hagigah commentary Maimonides gives us a list of the topics taken up in that divine science that is the content of *ma'aseh merkavah*: being as such, and transcendent entities (God, God as creator, angels, the soul, the intellect that cleaves to human beings, and what happens after death)[11]. In *Art of Logic* this subject matter is seen to be subsumed under theoretical philosophy. We have every indication, therefore, that Maimonides sees *ma'aseh merkavah* as the Jewish term for what the Aristotelian philosophers called "metaphysics."

In "Foundations of the Torah" Maimonides devotes chapters 3 and 4 to *ma'aseh bereshit* (as he says himself explicitly in IV.10). In these chapters he treats of the astronomical spheres, the stars, the four elements of sublunar matter, the process of generation and corruption, the relation of form and matter, and the nature of human beings. This latter discussion (IV. 8–9) is a consequence of the discussion of the relationship and form and matter since it mentions our ability to achieve transcendent existence after death.

In the *Guide* Maimonides tells us, "Thus we have mentioned there [in his legal compilations] that *ma'aseh bereshit* is identical with natural science (*al–im al–tabi'i*) and *ma'aseh merkavah* with divine science (*al–ilm al–ilahi*)" (I, Introduction, p. 6).

The other science, therefore, which deals with the principles of *gufei Torah* is physics. Physics and metaphysics, then, are the two sciences that constitute the principles upon which are based the specific *halakhot* of the Torah, the *gufei Torah*.[17]

We have other evidence that supports the thesis that Maimonides identified these sciences with the wisdom or science of the Torah. By way of explaining the purpose of the *Guide* Maimonides says (I, Introduction, p. 5):

> It is not the purpose of this Treatise to make its totality understandable to the vulgar or beginners in speculation, nor to teach those who have not engaged in any study other than the science of the Law—I mean the legalistic study of the Law[18] For the purpose of this Treatise and all those like it is the science of the Law in its true sense.

What is the "science of the Law in its true sense"?[19] Maimonides nowhere tells us exactly. A glance at the subject matter of the *Guide*, however (which includes God's attributes, his existence, unity, and incorporeality, the separate intellects, and *ma'aseh merkavah*) makes it hard to avoid the conclusion that this science is metaphysics. This idea is strengthened by the parallelism that may be seen to obtain between Maimonides's statement here in the *Guide* and his commentary on Hagigah II.1. He distinguishes here between "the

science of the Law in its true sense" on the one hand, and the
"legalistic study of the Law" on the other hand. The former
is the subject of the *Guide*, the latter, the subject of the *Mishneh Torah*.[20] This distinction parallels the distinction in the
Mishnah commentary between the "principles of *gufei Torah*"
(i.e., physics and metaphysics) and *gufei Torah* (i.e., the specific *halakhot* of the Torah). The principles of *gufei Torah*,
then, make up the "science of the Law in its true sense,"
which, in turn, is physics and metaphysics.[21]

This is not conclusive proof, however, that *hokhmat ha–Torah al ha–emet*, the "science of the Law in its true sense," is
metaphysics, or physics and metaphysics together, even if it
makes it very likely. Even the fact that Maimonides's medieval interpreters are unanimous in reading him in that way
(including Isaac Abravanel who, given his critique of Jewish
philosophy and Jewish philosophers, had every reason to
want to interpret Maimonides differently)[22] does not prove
that my interpretation is necessarily correct. Further evidence in support of this thesis, however, may be found in
another context.

"The Law as a whole," Maimonides informs us at the
beginning of *Guide* III.27 (p. 510), aims at two things: the
welfare of the soul and the welfare of the body. As for
the welfare of the soul, "it consists in the multitude's acquiring correct opinions corresponding to their respective
capacity." Between these two aims, "one is indubitably greater in nobility, namely the welfare of the soul—I mean the
procuring of correct opinions—while the second aim—I
mean the welfare of the body—is prior in nature and
time."[23] Maimonides goes on to define the welfare of the
soul:

> [Man's] ultimate perfection is to become rational *in actu;*
> this would consist in his knowing everything concerning all
> the beings that it is within the capacity of man to know in
> accordance with his ultimate perfection. It is clear that to
> this ultimate perfection there do not belong either actions
> or moral qualities[24] and that it consists only of opinions
> toward which speculation has led and that investigation has
> rendered compulsory. (p. 511)

The second perfection, the welfare of the soul, which we have just learned involves the apprehension of demonstratively proved scientific facts, presupposes the first perfection, the welfare of the body.[25] Having achieved the welfare of the body, however, we may then seek to achieve the second perfection "which is indubitably more noble and is the only cause of permanent preservation."

This issue is very important to Maimonides. That the Torah seeks to inculcate true opinions, over and above perfecting our social, moral, and ceremonial lives, is a sign of its divinity:

> If, on the other hand, you find a Law all of whose ordinances are due to attention being paid, . . . to the soundness of the circumstances pertaining to the body and also to the soundness of belief—a Law that takes pains to inculcate correct opinions with regard to God, may He be exalted, in the first place, and with regard to angels,[26] and that desires to make man wise, to give him understanding, and to awaken his attention, so that he should know the whole of that which exists in its true form—you must know that this guidance comes from Him, may He be exalted, and that this Law is divine.[27]

It is thus important for Maimonides to show that the Torah inculcates true doctrines; this proves that it is divine. That is what he is about in III.27 (and for much of the rest of that part of the *Guide*). Continuing our analysis of III.27, we find Maimonides affirming that

> the true Law then, which as we have already made clear is unique—namely the Law of Moses our Master—has come to bring us both perfections, I mean the welfare of the states of people in their relations with one another through the aboliton of reciprocal wrongdoing and through the acquisition of a noble and excellent character. . . . I mean also the soundness of the beliefs and the giving of correct opinions through which ultimate perfection is achieved. The letter of the Torah speaks of both perfections and informs us that the end of this Law in its entirety is the achievement of these two perfections. (p. 511)

The Torah, therefore is divine, for it not only seeks to improve our standards of behavior, but also imparts "correct opinions through which ultimate perfection is achieved."

Maimonides's position here in the *Guide* also finds clear expression in what is usually thought of as the most popular of his popular works, his "Epistle to Yemen." There he writes:

> Likewise, a person ignorant of the secrets of the revealed books and the inner significance of our Law will be led to believe that our religion has something in common with the established confessions [a reference to Islam and Christianity] if he makes a comparison between the two. For he will find that in the Torah there are prohibitions and commandments, and there are prohibitions and commandments in the others. . . . Yet if he could only fathom the inner meanings, he would realize that the essence of the Torah lies in the deeper meaning of its positive and negative precepts, every one of which will aid man in his striving after perfection and remove every impediment to the attainment of excellence. They will enable the masses and the elite to acquire moral and intellectual qualities, each according to his ability. Thus the godly community becomes preeminent, reaching a twofold perfection. By the first I mean man's leading his life in this world under the most agreeable and congenial conditions. The second will constitute the gain of the intelligibles, each in accordance with his native powers.[28]

Here, too, then, Maimonides is quite open about telling his reader that the Torah's truth is proved by the fact that it not only brings us to improved behavior, but causes us to "gain the intelligibles" by inculcating correct opinions.[29]

These correct opinions deal, in the first place, as we just saw in II.40, with God and the angels (i.e., the separate intellects). God and the angels are the primary topics of metaphysics. It seems, then, that the burden of argument must be on anyone who wishes to deny that the science of the Law in its true sense is metaphysics.

But of what importance is all this? Returning to the theme of our study, we now understand what sort of intellectual commitment underlies one's Maimonidean Judaism and why Maimonides was and had to be so welcoming with respect to conversion, why he expected all the Gentiles to become Jews in the messianic era, why he saw being Jewish first and foremost in terms of intellectual acquiescence to certain doctrines, and why he played down the special nature of the Jewish people. Metaphysics may be a difficult science, but it is not occult. Aristotle, a Greek pagan, came close to perfection in it. If the science of the Law in its true sense is indeed metaphysics, then there is no reason why a properly motivated Gentile cannot come to the science of the Law in its true sense and it must, therefore, be the case that when metaphysical knowledge ("knowledge of the Lord") becomes widespread, that conversion to Judaism will follow, or, at the very least, the difference between Jew and Gentile will no longer have any significance.[30]

Further evidence to this effect may be found in two remarkable statements of Maimonides's, one in the *Guide* and the other in the *Mishneh Torah*. *Guide* II.39 and II.40 represent a unit dealing with the legislative prophecy of Moses and the Torah.[31] In these chapters Maimonides sets out the form that an argument for the eternal validity of any putative divine law must take: if it can be shown that a particular claimant for the status of divine law is the most perfect possible exemplar of the class of bodies of law promulgated to govern societies, then it is eternally valid, for no other body of law can surpass it in perfection. In applying that test, Maimonides first distinguishes Mosaic prophecy from that of the Patriarchs and Moses' other predecessors. Moses alone called people to follow a body of law. Abraham, for example, "taught the people and explained to them *by means of speculative proofs* that the world has but one deity."[32] Moses, unlike Abraham, was a *legislative* as well as being a philosophical prophet. Furthermore, the burden of Moses' legislative prophecy, as is well-known, was addressed to an already constituted people (the descendants of Abraham), as opposed to the more purely philosophical prophecy of Abraham, which caused him to attempt to assemble a people. An indication of the perfection of the Torah of Moses is its equi-balance or justice (which Maimonides demonstrates in detail in part 3 of the *Guide*), it consisting of "manners of worship in which there is no burden or excess" (p. 380).

It is in connection with this last comment that Maimonides raises an objection to his thesis. There are those who find that the burdens of the Torah "are grievous, heavy, and difficult to bear." In response Maimonides says:

> The facility or difficulty of the Law should not be estimated with reference to the passions of the wicked, vile, morally corrupt men but should be considered with reference to the man who is perfect among the people. *For it is the aim of this Law that all human beings should be such a man.*[33]

It is the aim of the Torah, Maimonides tells us, in a chapter given over in large part to distinguishing the Torah prophecy of Moses from the prophecy of the Patriarchs, to bring *all human beings*[34] to the status of one "who is perfect among the people."

If this is the aim of the Torah, is it any surprise that when the world reaches messianic fulfillment, all human beings will be perfected by the Torah, and that in the meantime the Torah is understood in such a fashion (as being in the first place a body of metaphysical truths, supporting and supported by a body of commandments)[35] which makes conversion to Judaism open to all human beings and makes conversion an option to be welcomed?

The second text that supports this view is found in the thirteenth paragraph of the thirteenth chapter of the seventh book of the *Mishneh Torah*.[36] This is the very last paragraph in the *Book of Seeds* and thus, in structural terms, lies precisely at the midpoint of the *Mishneh Torah*, just before Maimonides opens his discussion of the laws governing the (messianic) temple service. I leave the significance of the doubled thirteen to the followers of Leo Strauss;[37] for my own part I cannot believe that the fact that this statement appears precisely in the middle of the *Mishneh Torah* is simple coincidence.

To the statement itself. Chapter 13 deals with the rights

of the Tribe of Levi concerning portions in the land of Israel. In paragraph 12 Maimonides had told us that the Levites had no inheritance in the land of Israel because they had been separated out for the service of God and were His special portion. "Not only the tribe of Levi," Maimonides says in paragraph 13,

> but also each and every individual of those who come into the world, whose spirit generously moves him and whose knowledge gives him understanding to set himself apart in order to serve before the Lord,[38] to serve Him, to worship Him, and to know Him, who walks upright as God had made him,[39] and releases his neck from the yoke of the many calculations that human beings are wont to pursue— such an individual is consecrated to the Holy of Holies, and his portion and inheritance shall be in the Lord forever and evermore. The Lord will grant him in this world whatsoever is sufficient for him, the same as he had granted to the priests and to the Levites. Thus indeed did David, upon whom be peace, say, *O Lord, the portion of mine inheritance and of my cup, Thou maintainest my lot.* (Ps. 16:5)[40]

Any human being then, who is moved by his or her spirit and knowledge to serve, worship, and know God, becomes sanctified like the holy of holies, achieves sustenance in this world and God becomes his or her portion and inheritance forever and ever (i.e., in the next world).

Once again, the hand of friendship and cooperation, more, the offer of physical support, shared worship, and shared life in the world to come, is extended to each and every human being who wishes to join himself or herself lto the worship of God.[41] The motivation for this step is explicitly posited in terms of knowledge and understanding. This being the case, this knowledge must in principle be available to all human beings. This, I submit, is further support of the claim just advanced whereby the science of the Law in its true sense is physics and metaphysics, sciences open in principle to all human beings.

That this statement comes before the laws describing the construction of the (messianic) temple gives some measure of further support to the argument made in chapter 5 that in the messianic era all human beings will ultimately become Jewish.

Before closing our discussion here note must be taken concerning one of the most vexed issues of Maimonidean hermeneutic, a famous text in "Laws of Kings," VIII.11. "Laws of Kings," VIII deals with the permitted behavior of Jewish soldiers, beginning with exceptions to the rules of *kashrut* and going on to a detailed exposition of the laws relating to the *yefat to'ar*, the beautiful captive.[42] Included in this discussion is the conversion of the beautiful captive to Judaism. That, in turn, leads to a discussion of the seven Noahide commandments. Maimonides then distinguishes between the *ger toshav*, the "resident alien," or "semiconvert" and the *hasid me–umot ha–olam*, the "righteous gentile."[43] The former is a Gentile who accepts the seven Noahide commandments. The latter is the subject of paragraph 11.

> All who accept the seven commandments and observes them scrupulously is a "righteous gentile," and will have a portion in the world to come, provided that he accepts them and performs them because the Holy One, blessed be He, commanded them in the Torah and made known through Moses, our teacher, that the observance thereof had been enjoined upon the descendents of Noah from antiquity. But if his observance thereof is based on a reasoned conclusion[44] he is not deemed a resident alien, or one of the righteous gentiles, *but* one of their wise men.[45]

The italicized "but" in the last sentence, for all its being a very small word, has generated the writing of many thousands of words. The Hebrew is *ela*. This is the reading of the vast majority of the *Mishneh Torah* manuscripts and at least one important early edition. Many of the printed editions, however, have another reading: *vi–lo*, which makes the last clause read, "and not one of their wise men." The difference in Hebrew between the letters *alef* and *vav* is minute; the difference here in meaning, vast. Much ink has been spilled and will no doubt continue to be spilled ("of the making of books there is no end") over the question of which reading is preferable. The problem is compounded by the fact that many interpreters have chosen this text as a hook on which to hang discussions concerning Maimonides's attitude to natural law.[46]

I have no intention of getting involved in the question of whether or not Maimonides adopted some theory or other of natural law. The question itself is in grave danger of being anachronistic and I am not at all convinced that it has bearing on the subject of my study here. On the other hand, the text in question might. Let us look at it.

Assuming that the *ela* (but) reading is correct we have no problem. Gentiles who arrive at an understanding of the Noahide laws on the basis of their reason, unaided by revelation, are wise. Whether or not they have a portion in the world to come is simply not an issue taken up by Maimonides here.[47]

But what if the *vi–lo* (and not) reading is correct? Does that pose problems for our interpretation of Maimonides? I think not. Maimonides distinguishes between the resident alien (*ger toshav*) and the righteous Gentile. He promises the latter a portion in the world to come and is silent about the eventual fate of the former, leading us to the supposition that what the resident alien earns is not a place in the world to come, but a place under Jewish sovereignty in this world.[48] The righteous Gentile earns a portion of the world to come only if he or she accepts the seven Noahide commandments because they are laid down in the Torah, that is, accepts the truth of Judaism. Strictly speaking, Maimonides cannot make this claim: it is his oft–repeated position that one's portion in the world to come depends upon one's measure of intellectual perfection. The best sense to be made of this, I think, is the following: a person whose intellect is truly perfected will, if he or she becomes acquainted with the Torah, recognize its divinity. This is the burden of Maimonides's comments quoted from *Guide* II.40 and III.27. Thus Maimonides can indeed promise such an individual a portion of the world to come.

On this basis the reading *vi–lo* is also acceptable. One who fails to recognize the wisdom of the Torah is not (*vi–lo*) truly wise. This does not mean that such a person has no portion in the world to come (the problem that caused Mendelssohn so much anguish); it is, I suppose, possible for one to perfect his or her intellect enough to achieve some small measure of immortality without having perfected it enough to recognize the divinity of the Torah, or one, like Aristotle, may have achieved a very high level of intellectual perfection, without, for historical reasons, ever having become acquainted with the Torah. Indeed, the case of Aristotle makes it clear that Maimonides did not mean to exclude intellectually perfected Gentiles who had not accepted the Noahide commandments from the world to come.

This last comment needs some explanation. In a well–known letter to Samuel ibn Tibbon Maimonides observes that there is no need for Samuel to study the writings of philosophers who preceded Aristotle because the works of the latter

> are sufficient by themselves and [superior] to all that were written before them. His intellect,[49] Aristotle's, is the extreme limit of human intellect, apart from him upon whom the divine emanation has flowed forth to such an extent that they[50] reach the level of prophecy, there being no level higher.[51]

We must further note that in *Guide* I.5 (p. 28) Maimonides calls Aristotle, "the chief of the philosophers."[52] Who were these philosophers of whom Aristotle is the chief? In a letter to the Sages of Montpellier[53] Maimonides writes that the *hakhamim*, wise men, of Greece, who were philosophers and "who are certainly wise," never dealt with astrology. In his commentary to Mishnah Avodah Zarah IV.7 Maimonides explains at length that the philosophers never dealt in astrology which, as he explains both there and in "Laws of Idolatry," I.1, is the cause and root of idolatry. Given all this, and that, as we saw in chapter 4, intellectual perfection is the necessary and sufficient condition for achieving a portion in the world to come, can there be any doubt that Maimonides assigned Aristotle a portion in the world to come?

On either reading (*ela* or *vi–lo*), therefore, "Laws of Kings," VIII.11 supports the interpretation of Maimonides offered in this book. A person who perfects his or her intellect will achieve a portion in the world to come, whether Jew or Gentile. Gentiles who achieve this level of intellectual perfection and become acquainted with the Torah will recognize its divinity. They may then go on to become full converts or (if they do not wish to become part of the Jewish people) take advantage of the Noahide option and become one of the "righteous among the gentiles." Either way, the key is the recognition that first and foremost the "science of the Torah" in the true sense is science (physics and metaphysics) and, as such, is open to all rational beings.

Under the heading "the nature of Torah" we have discussed in this chapter those views the adoption of which in effect make one Jewish according to Maimonides. Being Jewish is not a matter of "essences" or inherent, inborn characteristics; it is a matter, in the first instance, of the adoption of certain views, and, in the second instance, the satisfaction of certain formal conditions. Analyzing texts from a variety of sources—the commentary on Mishnah Hagigah, *Art of Logic*, "Laws of the Foundations of the Torah," and the *Guide of the Perplexed*—we have shown that Maimonides identifies *ma'aseh merkavah* with metaphysics, *ma'aseh bereshit* with physics, and the two together as the "principles" of the specific *halakhot* of the Torah. I then showed that it is these sciences, especially metaphysics, which Maimonides had in mind when he spoke of the "science of the Torah in its true sense." I did this on the basis of his claim in *Guide* III.27 that the Torah teaches both actions and true views. These views, we learn in II.40, deal with God and the angels, the primary subjects of metaphysics. The science of the Torah, then, is metaphysics. Now, metaphysics may be a difficult science, but it is not occult or esoteric. Normal human beings who apply themselves can master it to one degree or another. The "depth content" of the Torah, therefore, is not some secret teaching accessible only to certain initiates (as in versions of Jewish mysticism) but is open in principle to all human beings. We see here another consequence of Maimonides's philosophical psychology: since Jews are not born with special equipment that makes it possible for them to decipher the Torah, as it were, such decipherment must, in principle, be possible for all human beings. We have seen here that it is. Texts that support this reading of Maimonides were examined and his statement in "Laws of Kings," VIII.11, over which there is so much debate, was shown to support our reading, either way the text is read.

9

Israel

Maimonides's attitude toward the Jewish People ("Israel" in his terminology) was one of great national pride. He
was convinced that the Jews, as a national group, were in
every way superior to other national groups.[1] Unlike Halevi,
however, he did not make an entire metaphysic out of this
pride. The superiority of the Jews derived from two sources:
God's promise to Abraham that his progeny would enjoy
special benefits and, most importantly, the Torah.[2]

Maimonides's comments on the nature of the Jewish
people mirror these two sources of Jewish superiority. The
Jews are on the one hand a people, defined by their descent
from Abraham and, on the other hand, a community defined by the Torah. While both these understandings of the
Jewish people find expression in Maimonides's writings, the
latter is much more important than the former. It is my
intent in this chapter to prove this last claim and explain its
significance.

Note should be made of the fact that in this case, as with
many of the others discussed in this book, Maimonides chose
between options presented to him by rabbinic literature. In
the Midrash, for example, we read, "For had it not been for
My Torah which you have accepted, I would not recognize you or look upon you more than any other idol-
worshippers."[3] This may be contrasted with statements such

as, "Even though they [the Jews] are unclean, the Divine Presence is among them."[4]

In order to make my discussion clearer, I will introduce a distinction that is not textually grounded in Maimonides's writings, but that will help us keep in mind the twofold nature of his writings about the Jews. Those individuals constituted as a national group by their shared descent from Abraham I will call "Jews," while that religious group constituted by its adherence to the Torah I will call "Israel." Maimonides was not always careful to keep these two meanings distinct and may even have occasionally inadvertently fudged them. The distinction is in any event hard to keep sharp since in historical and *halakhic* terms "the Jews" and "Israel" denote the same entity. Despite all this, ignoring the distinction makes understanding Maimonides very difficult.

Indirect but compelling evidence to the effect that Maimonides adopted the distinction here outlined can be found in "Laws of Kings," X.8.

> The Rabbis said that the sons of Keturah, who are of the seed of Abraham, who came after Ishmael and Isaac, are obligated to be circumcised. But since today the descendants of Ishmael have become intermingled with the descendants of Keturah, all of them are obligated to be circumcised on the eighth day, but are not executed because of it.[5]

Here we have a *commandment*, not one of the seven Noahide laws, devolving upon a group of non–Jews because of their Abrahamic descent. The commandment of circumcision was given to Abraham and to his descendants (Gen. 17:9–14). Maimonides takes that literally and imposes upon the Ishmaelites (Muslims), who had married into the descendants of Abraham, the obligation to circumcise their children on the eighth day after birth (as mandated by Gen. 17:12). Can there be clearer proof to the effect that Maimonides distinguishes between Abrahamic descent on the one hand from membership in the people of Israel on the other hand?[6]

Just as Maimonides refused to accept an essentialist definition of who an individual Israelite is, as we saw in chapter

4, he also rejects essentialist definitions of Israel the people. Maimonides never denies, indeed he is eager to affirm, that the Jews should be proud of their Abrahamic descent and that this descent confers great benefits upon them. But, withal, Maimonides repeatedly affirms that what makes Israel Israel is the Torah and not any inborn characteristic, inherent quality, or shared biological origin.

We can see this in many ways. First, in his letters to Obadiah the Proselyte, as we saw above, Maimonides emphasizes the importance of commitment to Torah over and above actual physical descent from Abraham. "Let not your lineage be base in your eyes, for if we link our lineage to Abraham, Isaac, and Jacob, you link your lineage to He Who spoke and the world came into being."[7]

Examining Maimonides's comments on the nature of the activities of Abraham himself is also illuminating. In "Laws of Idolatry," I.1 and 2 Maimonides explains how humankind, originally monotheist, fell into error (literally) and began to worship idols. "The world moved on in this fashion," Maimonides says in I.2,

> till that pillar of the world, the patriarch Abraham, was born. After he was weaned . . . his mind began to reflect. . . . "How is it possible that this sphere should continuously be guiding the world, and have no one to guide it and cause it turn round; for it cannot be that it turns round of itself?" He had no teacher . . . but his mind was busily working and reflecting till he had attained the way of truth and apprehended the correct line on the basis of his own correct intellect and knew that there is one God, that He guides the sphere, that He created everything, and that among all that exists there is no god beside Him.[8]

Abraham, then, is presented as a natural philosopher who came to recognize that God exists, is one, and created the world, on the basis of his unaided reason.[9] What then did Abraham do? He tried to convince his neighbors, rationally, of their error.

> He realized that the whole world was in error. . . . Having attained this *knowledge* he began to *refute* the inhabitants of

Ur of the Chaldees, *arguing* with them . . . and com-
menced to instruct the people. . . . When he prevailed over
them with his *arguments*, the king sought to slay
him . . . when the people flocked to him and questioned
him regarding his assertions, he would instruct each one
according to his *intellect*, until he had returned them to the
way of truth.[10]

Abraham, having achieved philosophical certainty, sought to
share his knowledge and certainty with others, by way of
rational argumentation.

Maimonides presents a similar picture in the *Guide of the
Perplexed*, although there the emphasis is on distinguishing
the Patriarchs, who sought rationally to convince their fellows of the truths of God's existence, unity and creation,
from Moses, who brought the Torah that includes these
truths but also includes commandments and was sent by
God. Moses was distinguished from the Patriarchs because
he was able to "make a claim to prophecy on the ground that
God had spoken to him and sent him on a mission." The
Patriarchs, however,

were addressed in regard to their private affairs only; I
mean only in regard to their perfection, their right guidance concerning their actions, and the good tidings for
them concerning the position their descendants would
attain.[11]

Unlike Moses, who came with commandments from God, the
Patriarchs "addressed a call to people by means of speculation and instruction." Once again we see that Abraham, Isaac, and Jacob[12] came to know God on the basis of rational,
philosophical grounds and sought to share the truth thus
discovered with their contemporaries. Thanks to this, God
promised their descendants many benefits.

The same point is reiterated in *Guide* II.39. Protecting
the uniqueness of the Torah, Maimonides asserts the
uniqueness of Mosaic prophecy. No other prophet has ever
said to a group of people, "God has sent me to you and
commanded me to say to you such and such things; He has

forbidden you to do such and such things and commanded you to do such and such things." Prophets other than Moses,

> who received a great overflow, as for instance Abraham, assembled the people and called them by way of teaching and instruction to adhere to the truth that he had grasped. Thus Abraham taught the people and *explained to them by means of speculative proofs* that the world has but one deity, that He has created all the things that are other than Himself, and that none of the forms and no created thing in general ought to be worshipped.[13]

The founder of the Jewish nation, then, is presented in both the *Mishneh Torah* and the *Guide of the Perplexed* as a philosopher who achieved knowledge of God through rational examination of the world around him and sought rationally to convince others of the truths he had discovered. This is made clear here in this passage from the *Guide*. Abraham received an "overflow" (i.e., emanation) from God, such an emanation, as Maimonides explains in his chapters on prophecy (II.32–48), being a consequence of intellectual perfection. As a reward, Abraham was promised that special benefits would be conferred upon his progeny. The foundation of the Jewish people as an entity defined in terms of its Abrahamic descent is itself a consequence of a philosophical appreciation of God.

Maimonides's explanation of how the descendants of Abraham were constituted into the entity called Israel is particularly illuminating. We saw that Maimonides compares the creation of Israel with the process of conversion: "With three things did Israel enter the covenant: circumcision, immersion, and sacrifice . . . and so it is for all generations, when a gentile wishes to enter the covenant and shelter under [lit. stand at the threshold of] the wings of the Shekhinah, and accept upon himself the yoke of Torah, he needs circumcision, immersion, and the bringing of a sacrifice."[14] As we also saw, Maimonides makes the essential element of conversion to be the acceptance of (philosophical) teachings concerning God.[15] I do not think that it is pressing the issue too much to impute to Maimonides the view that the philosophical acceptance of the existence and unity of God was no less essential to the mass "conversion" of the Jews from the Tribe of Abraham to the People of Israel at Sinai than it is for the conversion of individuals through the ages.

This interpretation of Maimonides is strengthened by his account of the theophany at Sinai. Maimonides denied that all the Jews prophesied at Sinai,[16] but he did insist that the assembled people rationally understood the philosophical import of the first two statements in the Decalogue. "It is clear to me," Maimonides says, opening *Guide* II.33, "that at the gathering at Mt. Sinai, not everything that reached Moses also reached all Israel. Speech was addressed to Moses alone . . . and he, peace upon him, went to the foot of the mountain and communicated to the people what he had heard" (pp. 363–64). The people of Israel did not then share Moses' prophetic apprehension. But in explaining the rabbinic dictum to the effect that Israel heard the first two statements of the Decalogue directly from the "mouth" of God,[17] Maimonides says:

> They mean that these words reached them just as they reached Moses our Master and that it was not Moses our Master who communicated them to them. For these two principles, I mean the existence of the deity and his being one,[18] are knowable by human speculation alone. Now with regard to everything that can be known by demonstration, the status of the prophet and that of everyone else who knows it are equal; there is no superiority of one over the other. These two principles are not known through prophecy alone. The text of the Torah says, *Unto thee it was shown*[19] (Deut. 4:35). As for the other commandments, they belong to the class of generally accepted opinions and those adopted in virtue of tradition, not to the class of the intellecta. (p. 364)

Here we are told by Maimonides that Israel at Sinai apprehended by philosophical demonstration the truth of precisely those two principles (God's existence and unity) which are taught to the convert and by virtue of the acceptance of which he or she becomes a proselyte to Judaism. Israel became Israel by virtue of its acceptance of these two principles. This is convincing proof of my assertion concerning the congruence between the process of conversion and the creation of Israel. At the moment of its inception, therefore, Israel was constituted as such by the rational acceptance of true philosophical teachings concerning God. This is as far from an essentialist definition of Israel as one can get!

The same point becomes clear when we examine how individuals are excluded from *Klal Yisrael*, the community of Israel. As we saw, Maimonides asserts that "anyone who destroys one of these foundations which I have explained to you [Maimonides's 'thirteen principles'] has left the community of Torah adherents."[20] I alluded to the harsh penalties Maimonides imposes on the heretic, sectarian, and *epikoros*.[21] Here perhaps I ought to elaborate on that subject in some detail. In "Laws of Repentance," III.7 Maimonides defines a sectarian as one who denies any of the first five of his thirteen principles of faith. In "Laws of Idolatry," II.5 he affirms that "Israelite sectarians are not like Israelites at all" and that it is forbidden to converse with them or return their greeting. He compares them to idolators and says that even if they repent they are never accepted back into the community. The *epikoros* is defined in "Repentance," III.8 as one who denies prophecy, Mosaic prophecy, and God's knowledge. In "Laws of the Murderer," IV.10 and in "Laws of Mourning," I.10 Maimonides informs us that the *epikoros* is not considered part of the community of Israel; in the latter place we are bidden not to mourn them on their deaths. We are encouraged to destroy them in "Laws of Idolatry," X.1 and told that they are no better than informers, the lowest of the low in Jewish estimation. That the *epikoros* has no place in the world to come is the burden of "Laws of Testimony," XI.10; we are also informed there that it goes without saying that their testimony is not acceptable in a court, since they are not Israelites at all. In this paragraph we are bidden to kill the *epikoros*.[22] The parallelism here is compelling: one exits the community of Israel by *denying* certain teachings parallel to the way in which that community was constituted: through the rational *acceptance* of certain (philosophical) teachings.[23]

Further evidence of Maimonides's nonessentialist understanding of the nature of the community of Israel can be found, of all places, in his "Epistle to Yemen." I say, "of all places," because this text was written in order to bolster the confidence of a Jewish community suffering from Muslim persecution. Part of Maimonides's strategy here is to denigrate the Muslims and praise the Jews. That, at least, appears to be what he is doing at first glance. In actuality, he denigrates *Islam* and praises *Judaism*. Even in this context, then, his nonessentialist approach to the definition of Israel comes to the fore.

Maimonides starts that part of his discussion relevant to our question by citing Deut. 10:15. *Yet it was to your fathers that the Lord was drawn in His love for them, so that He chose you, their lineal descendants, from among all the peoples.* That verse could be used to underline an essentialist definition of the nature of the Jewish people, distinguishing them from all other peoples by virtue of their lineal descent from Abraham. But Maimonides uses it for other purposes, explaining "that ours is the true and divine religion, revealed to us through Moses, chief of the former as well as the later prophets. By means of it, God has distinguished us from the rest of mankind."[24] This choice, Maimonides goes on to say after citing Deut. 10:15, "was not made thanks to our merits, but was rather an act of grace, on account of our ancestors who were *cognizant* of God and obedient to Him" (pp. 96–97).

Maimonides further emphasizes the point under discussion here: "Since God has singled us out by His law and precepts, and our preeminence over the others was manifested in His rules and statutes" (p. 97). Israel was singled out by the Torah, not by anything inherent in its collective or individual character. Israel is indeed superior to other nations, not because of some inborn quality, but because of the rules and statutes of the Torah.

Maimonides's approach to this question comes out even in his discussion of how other nations sought to attack the Jews. It was not a matter of what we today would call anti–Semitism or Jew hatred, but a matter of anti–Torahism and anti–Judaism. Jealous of Jewish preeminence (a consequence of the Torah),

all the nations, instigated by envy and impiety, rose up
against us in anger, and all the kings of the earth, motivated by injustice and enmity applied themselves to per-
secute us. They wanted to thwart God, but He will not be
thwarted. Ever since the time of revelation every despot or
rebel ruler, be he violent or ignoble, *has made it his first aim
and final purpose to destroy our Law, and to vitiate our religion*
by means of the sword, by violence, or by brute force. Such
were Amalek, Sisera, Sennacherib, Nebuchadnezzar,
Titus, Hadrian, and others like them.[25]

Attacks on the Jews, that is, are really attacks on Judaism.

There is one place in the "Epistle to Yemen" where
heavy emphasis is placed on Abrahamic descent. It is also
one of the few (perhaps only) places in his writings that
Maimonides makes explicit reference to the notion of the
chosen people.[26] "When God spoke to Abraham He made it
amply clear that all the blessings that He promised and all his
children to whom He will reveal the Law and whom He will
make the Chosen People—all this is meant only for the seed
of Isaac. Ishmael is regarded as an adjunct and appendage in
the blessings of Isaac." Three points must be made. First, the
immediate context of this passage, and the passage itself,
make clear that Maimonides is primarily interested in refuting the Muslim claim that the favored son of Abraham was
Ishmael, not Isaac. Second, it is reasonable to read this passage as saying that Israel will become the chosen people because of the fact that the Torah will be revealed to them, not
because of some inherent essence or nature of the Jews.
Third, it is true—the Jews did receive the Torah, and thus
became constituted as the faith community of Israel, as a
reward to Abraham; but this in no way implies that the Jews
as such are qualitatively different from other peoples.

There is one last place in the "Epistle to Yemen" that
supports the reading of Maimonides offered here. Toward
the end of the work Maimonides expresses a messianic wish.
Referring to the Jews of Yemen, he says, "May God increase
your numbers and hasten the day of gathering you with the
entire *religious community.*"[27] Even in the context of a prayer

for the messianic ingathering Maimonides makes reference to a *religious community* (defined, we have seen over and over, in terms of its having accepted the Torah) and not to a *people* defined in some essential fashion or other.

I noted that Maimonides rarely makes reference to the notion of the chosen people. This alone is suggestive. While the Torah plays a central role in his thought and finds central expression in his "Thirteen Principles"[28] the notion of the chosen people is almost entirely absent from his writings and plays no role whatsoever in the "Thirteen Principles" or in the "Laws of the Foundations of the Torah." Indeed, in that latter work, as noted, the term *Israel* shows up for the first time only at the end of chapter 4.

Further illustration of this point can be had by examining Maimonides's use of biblical verses which form the basis for the notion of the chosen people. I examined a variety of these verses (Gen. 18:1, 18:18–19, Exod. 19:5–6, and Deut. 7:6–8, 14:2, 18:5). Some of them Maimonides never discussed, and others are used in ways that throw no light on Maimonides's ideas concerning the nature of the Jewish people. Usages that are relevant, however, invariably support the interpretation of Maimonides here put forward (as is exemplified by his use of Deut. 10:15 in "Epistle to Yemen," just discussed). A number of examples will make this clear. One of the earliest expressions of the idea of the chosen people is Gen. 18:18–19.

> And Abraham shall surely become a great and mighty nation, and all the nations of the earth shall be blessed in him. For I have known him, to the end that he may command his children and his household after him, that they may keep the way of the Lord, to do righteousness and justice; to the end that the Lord may bring upon Abraham that which He hath spoken of Him.

According to Rav Kafih's index of biblical citations in his works, Maimonides makes no reference at all to Gen. 18:18 while verse 19 is cited seven times.[29] While some of these citations have nothing to do with the issue under discussion, others are most suggestive.

Thus, Maimonides opens the last chapter of "Laws of
Gifts to the Poor" (X.1) by telling the reader that one must
observe the commandment of charity more scrupulously
than any other positive commandment, "for charity is the
sign of the righteous seed of Abraham, our Father, as it says
*For I have known him to the end that he may command his
children . . . to give charity*[30] and neither can the seat of Israel
be firm nor the true religion stand without charity." Here we
have the "righteous seed of Abraham" referred to and even
characterized by a special characteristic: charity. But Maimonides immediately explains that the seed of Abraham are
not intrinsically charitable; rather, they are *commanded* to give
charity; it was because they were going to receive that commandment that they became constituted as the "righteous
seed of Abraham" and it is by fulfillment of that commandment that they are recognized as such. The persuasive nature of Maimonides's argument here is clear as well. He is
trying to encourage the Jews to give charity; did they do so
naturally, thanks to some intrinsic character, his argument
would be otiose.[31]

Our verse shows up four times in the *Guide*. In II.39 (p.
379) it is used to show that Abraham did not convey God's
commandments to his household. In III.24 (p. 502) Maimonides cites the verse to support his claim that "Abraham our
Father was the first to make known the belief in Unity, to
establish prophecy, and to perpetuate this opinion and draw
people to it." In III.43 (p. 572) it is explained that the descendants of the Patriarchs enjoy benefits thanks to the
promises God made to their forbears. These promises, in
turn, were made because Abraham, Isaac, and Jacob "were
perfect people in their opinions and their moral character."
In the last citation of the verse in the *Guide* (III.51, p. 624),
we are reminded that the Patriarchs sought "to bring into a
being a religious community[32] that would know and worship
God"—a religious *community*, not a *people* defined by some
essential characteristic, and a community defined by its mission: to know and worship God.

Maimonides also cites the verse in his first letter to
Obadiah the Proselyte.[33] We have discussed that letter in

some detail and have already shown how it opposes any possibility of reading Maimonides as one who holds that the
Jewish people have some inherent, essential characteristic
that distinguishes them from other nations. In the particular
context under discussion Maimonides uses the verse to support his contention that all those who adopt Judaism are of
the household of Abraham.

Our review of Maimonides's use of Gen. 18:19, then,
confirms the thesis just proposed: Maimonides plays down
the notion of the chosen people, denies that the Jews have
any inherent, essential characteristic that distinguish them
prima facie from other nations, and emphasizes instead the
importance of the community of Israel as constituted by
the Torah, which in turn means the rational acceptance of
the philosophical truths of God's existence and unity.

A further example is Exod. 19:5–6.

> Now therefore if ye will hearken unto My voice indeed,
> and keep My covenant then ye shall be Mine own treasure
> from among all the peoples; for all the earth is Mine. And
> ye shall be unto me a kingdom of priests, and a holy nation.

Here is Maimonides's comment (*Guide* III.32, p. 526, emphasis added):

> For a sudden transition from one opposite to another is
> impossible. And therefore man, according to his nature, is
> not capable of abandoning suddenly all to which he was
> accustomed. As therefore God sent Moses our Master *to
> make out of us* "a kingdom of priests and a holy nation"—
> *through the knowledge of Him.*

Israel, then, is *made* into a holy nation (i.e., it is not intrinsically or inherently holy), through its being taught by Moses
correct knowledge concerning God. Here we see again, in
the clearest possible fashion, that there is nothing inherently
or essentially special or unique about Israel; it is the rational
appropriation of metaphysical truths about God that con-
stitutes Israel as a "kingdom of priests and holy nation."[34]
Other evidence for Maimonides's nonessentialist inter-

pretation of the Jewish people is found in a text that seems, at first reading, to teach the opposite. At the end of a discussion of certain astronomical phenomena, and, more importantly and immediately, a discussion of the nature and activities of the separate intellects (*Guide* II.11, p. 276), Maimonides points out that he had already explained that "all these views do not contradict anything said by our prophets and the sustainers of our Law. For our community[35] is a community that is full of knowledge and is perfect, as He, may He be exalted, has made clear through the intermediary of the Master who made us perfect, saying *Surely, this great nation[36] is a wise and understanding people"* (Deut. 4:6). Here we have a text in which Maimonides says that the Jewish nation or people is "full of knowledge and perfect." Does this not run counter to the reading of Maimonides urged here, according to which the Jewish people, in and of itself, as what we today would call an "ethnic entity," has no special, inherent, essential characteristics?

Actually, not only does this text not run counter to my thesis, it strengthens it. When Maimonides says that the Jews are "full of knowledge and perfect" he means that they are full of knowledge and *therefore* perfect. This is proved by the sequel.

> However, when the wicked from among the ignorant nations ruined our good qualities, destroyed our words of wisdom and our compilations, and caused our men of knowledge to perish, so that we again became ignorant, as we had been threatened because of our sins—for it says: *And the wisdom of their wise men shall perish, and the understanding of their prudent men shall be hid* (Isa. 29:14); when, furthermore, we mingled with these nations and their opinions were taken over by us, as were their morals and actions . . . when, in consequence of all this, we grew up accustomed to the opinions of the ignorant, these philosophic views appeared to be, as it were, foreign to our Law, just as they are foreign to the opinions of the ignorant. However, matters are not like this.

We see here that the perfection of Israel is not an inborn characteristic, but a consequence of their knowledge. When that knowledge is corrupted through assimilation to ignorant and immoral nations, the Jews behave as foolishly and wickedly as those who have influenced them.[37] We further see here that it is the philosophical views embodied in the Torah that make of the Jews a "wise and understanding people." This is seen by the context of our discussion here in II.11 and by the conclusion of the passage just quoted. It is because of our having grown accustomed to the opinions of the ignorant that the philosophical views discussed in II.11 appeared foreign to the Torah. Had the Jews understood that these views were not foreign to the Torah, they would still be a "wise and understanding people."

I have shown here that Maimonides, in effect, distinguishes the ethnic grouping defined in the first instance through Abrahamic descent from the faith community Israel, defined in the first instance by its acceptance of certain true philosophical views. Texts discussed included Maimonides's letters to Obadiah the Proselyte, his discussions of Abraham the philosopher in both the *Mishneh Torah* and the *Guide of the Perplexed*, and Maimonides's argument to the effect that the Jews (the seed of Abraham) became Israel through a process of conversion that involved the acceptance of certain philosophical teachings. We further saw that exclusion from Israel, like joining it, depends upon the holding of certain views (in this case, heretical ones). Maimonides's dramatically nonessentialist reading of the nature of the Jewish people was supported through an analysis of texts from his "Epistle to Yemen," his near total avoidance of the notion of the "chosen people," and his use of Gen. 18:19 and Exod. 19:5–6, verses ordinarily interpreted as supporting an essentialist reading of the nature of Israel.

Maimonides's understanding of the nature of the people of Israel, like his understanding of ethics, prophecy, providence, and immortality, his conception of the place of Gentiles in the messianic era, his approach to proselytes and proselytisation, his understanding of dogma, and his understanding of the nature of the Torah, is a further consequence of his having adopted the psychological theory according to which human beings are born equally ignorant and equally capable of overcoming that ignorance.[38] Once again, we have seen Maimonides adopt a particular and, in this case as in the others, unusual position on a narrowly "religious" issue because of his antecedent adoption of a philosophical claim.[39]

10

Conclusion

What I have done here is to examine a number of what can be called "narrowly" religious issues on which Maimonides has taken stands that put him outside of the concensus of the traditional Judaism of which he was an heir and to which he contributed so much. I have examined five matters in detail—the place of Gentiles in the messianic era, the nature of conversion and the attitude Jews ought to take toward proselytes, the relationship between dogma and Jewishness, the nature of Jewish faith, and the nature of the Jewish people—and some others (prophecy, providence, and immortality) in a more cursory fashion. In each case I have shown that Maimonides's position on what would ordinarily be called a strictly religious matter can best be understood in the light of his antecedent adoption of a particular philosophical view of human nature.[1]

According to that view, human beings are born with a capacity or potential to learn. When we are born, we are not yet fully human. Only if we actualize our potential to apprehend intelligibles do we actually become human beings. A consequence of this position is that Maimonides is given no way in which to distinguish Jews from Gentiles at birth. Contrary to Halevi and the *Zohar*, according to Maimonides *ab initio* we are all basically the same. Another way of putting this is to say that were Maimonides aware of the "nature

versus nurture" controversy, he would opt for the nurture
over nature approach, insisting that what we ultimately become depends more on what we do with ourselves than on
what is given us at birth. Jew and Gentile, that is, are distinguished more by the way in which they are nurtured, and
importantly, nurture themselves, than they are by any natural endowments. Only those individuals who come to adopt
the doctrines taught by the Torah (and, having adopted
these doctrines come to understand the necessity for obedience to the commandments of the Torah) fully realize
themselves as Jews. The adoption of these doctrines is open
to any one. There is, thus, no a priori reason why *any* human
being should be barred from fully converting to Judaism, as
all will do in the messianic era, when the earth will be full of
the knowledge of God. Similarly, in answering the related
questions, who is a proper Jew and who will be admitted to
the world to come, Maimonides phrases his response in
purely theological terms. Let it be well–understood. There
are two transitions where one's religious status is absolutely
crucial: at the point where one "joins" the religion, and at the
point where one seeks admittance to the world to come.
Maimonides could not change the entrenched understanding that one becomes a Jew by being born to a Jewish mother.
In cases where the matter was more fluid, and in which he
therefore could make determinations (i.e., the questions of
conversion, of being considered a proper [nonheretical] Jew,
and of admittance to the world to come) Maimonides insisted
on the acceptance of doctrine as the essential factor.[2]

It was shown in the second chapter of this study that
Maimonides adopts the psychological theory here imputed
to him in both his *halakhic* and philosophical works. Should
one desire further evidence to that effect, it is offered by his
positions on ethics, prophecy, providence, immortality, the
messianic era, conversion, dogma, the nature of Jewish faith,
and the nature of the Jewish people. There is a give–and–
take here, a back and forth flow to the argument. Once
having seen Maimonides's view on human nature, we understand why he had to adopt his positions on the messianic era,
conversion, dogma, the Torah, and Israel. That he in fact

adopted those positions is further evidence (though it is hardly needed) to the effect that he indeed adopted the psychological theory that he in fact adopted. What has developed here, then, is important evidence to the effect that in Maimonides's works there is an essential congruity between his philosophical and religious positions.[3] Philosophical positions (in this case, psychology) determine religious stands. This is to say that on many issues the Jewish tradition offered Maimonides choices, choices between what we would today call particularist and universalist positions. He consistently seems to adopt the latter over the former. What I have tried to show is that in the cases under study here he did so because of his philosophical orientation. Let this be well understood. Maimonides did not pick and choose those elements of the tradition congenial to him, selectively quoting this text here, subtly and consciously reshaping that tradition there. The tradition itself offered him options on many (but, of course, not all) issues; having adopted a particular philosophical orientation, he was enabled to weave a consistent whole out of the panopoly of Jewish views available to him.

We add here, then, further support for a unified view of Maimonides and undermine the opposed view, according to which there are unresolved contradictions between the (sincerely held) views of Maimonides the philosopher and the expressed views of Maimonides the rabbi. Our discussion also supports the view that Maimonides the rabbi must be understood in terms of Maimonides the philosopher. Thus Maimonides, the "culturally Spanish–Arab" philosopher[4] and disciple of Al–Farabi,[5] for whom *halakhah* was an avocation,[6] disappears, as does the Maimonides recreated in the image of late nineteenth– and early twentieth–century Eastern European yeshiva heads, for whom philosophy was at best a concession to contemporary trends of thought.

Another way of putting this is a follows. There are two widely accepted ways of viewing Maimonides. One may be called vertical, the other horizontal. On the first view, Maimonides is situated in the chain of Jewish tradition stretching back to Moses and is seen primarily as an *halakhic* decisor. It is primarily with respect to that tradition that Maimonides's views are studied and understood. On the second view, Maimonides is situated in the context of contemporary or near–contemporary Muslim philosophy and it is with respect to thinkers like Al–Farabi that Maimonides's views are studied and understood. The correct interpretation is that Maimonides must be understood as standing at the nexus of two vectors, the vertical one stretching back to Moses and the horizontal one encompassing his philosophical contemporaries and near contemporaries. Maimonides was convinced that one could and must live in both these worlds simultaneously.

The claim I am urging here is that while Maimonides interpreted Judaism philosophically, he did not consciously reject it. This is the interpretation of Maimonides defended in my *Maimonides on Human Perfection*. He may have adopted views on prophecy, providence, creation, etcetera, at variance with received opinions in the Jewish world, but these are views that he thought were truly taught by the Torah. This approach to Maimonides has recently been reiterated by Yizhak Twersky, one of its most eminent supporters, in connection with philosophical themes in the *Mishneh Torah*:

> It seems to me that the inference from this is not that the philosophic or extra–halakhic dimension in the *Mishneh Torah* is meager and tenuous, but rather that it is imperceptibly interwoven and fully integrated into the very texture of the code. It is so natural and so integral that it need not be singled out or stamped or otherwise identified. Such themes as creation, prophecy, free will, providence, eschatology, history of religion, magic and medicine, and, of course, political theory and ethical theory are treated in the *Mishneh Torah* and not characterized as individual, personal opinions; they are presented anonymously and authoritatively, as flowing necessarily and incontrovertiblty from the universally recognized sources. The source and its interpretation or amplification form an harmonious mosaic, a seamless web.[7]

A further upshot of our discussion is a clearer understanding of Maimonides's views on the nature of Jewish identity. What is it that makes one a Jew? The tradition seems to offer two choices. One can hold that there is something inherent in one's very nature that makes one a Jew. On such a view, which I have called an "essentialist" position, there is some metaphysical or mystical essence that inheres in every Jew, by virtue of which he is a Jew. This view explains why it is that, as with the mafia, one cannot "resign" from Judaism. It has difficulty explaining how it is that Gentiles can convert to Judaism and has difficulty in dealing with the universalistic accounts of the end of days found in many of the prophetic works. Maimonides, we have seen, must and does reject this view.

On the alternative view, being Jewish is first and foremost a matter of *commitment*. On my understanding of Maimonides, that commitment involves the intellectual acquiescence to certain doctrines. Once the nature of being Jewish is understood in terms of the acceptance of certain views, we once again see clearly why Maimonides could not but view conversion in a basically positive light, anticipate that in the end of days all humans would become Jews, define both adherence to Judaism and admission to the world to come in terms of the acceptance of certain universally accessible (philosophical) views, and define the Jewish People ("Israel"), not in ethnic terms, but in terms of the acceptance of those views.

Reviewing the argument presented here in greater detail, in the first chapter I presented two views on what it means to be a Jew. According to certain *midrashim*, Halevi, and the *Zohar*, Jews all have some kind of inborn, inherent characteristic by virtue of which they are "essentially," not "accidentally" distinguished from non–Jews. I pointed out that this view found Plato's theory of the soul congenial. Aristotelian theories of the soul, on the other hand, such as that adopted by Maimonides (as I showed in the second chapter) commit one to the position that basically human beings are all alike. What distinguishes them is not some inherent quality, but the quality and quantity of what they know.

Consistent with his philosophical psychology, Maimonides adopts a theory of ethics according to which human beings at birth are like a clear slate, upon which education, training, and acculturation write out their moral characters. All humans are born with basically the same moral potential and the same absence of fully formed character traits. This being the case, moral qualities that we have acquired can be changed if we are willing to work at it, especially if we avail ourselves of the guidance of the wise, the "physicians of the souls." Obedience to the Torah leads to high moral virtue; in this sense Jews, Maimonides held, are morally superior to Gentiles. But that is a matter of education, not inborn character.

This philosophical psychology forces Maimonides to adopt a number of unusual positions on questions of a more narrowly religious or parochial nature. Among these are the subject matter of chapter 4, providence, prophecy, and immortality. In each case we have seen that for Maimonides the simple fact that one is a Jew plays no role in determining whether one will enjoy God's providence, will prophesy, or will reach the world to come. In each case it is intellectual perfection that is crucial.

Chapter 5 examines another such issue: the question of the status of Gentiles in the messianic era. Many Jewish authorities assume that until the end of days the distinction between Jew and Gentile will remain; after the Messiah's coming, the Jews will rule the Gentiles who at present rule them. Maimonides, I showed, rejected this view, anticipating a time when all Gentiles would become Jews, either through formal conversion, as I maintain, or because the distinction would cease to be relevant, as Ya'akov Blidstein maintains. This position was made both possible and necessary by Maimonides's philosophical psychology. Since all human beings will devote themselves to the pursuit of the knowledge of God in the messianic era, that which truly distinguishes Gentiles from Jews will disappear.

Similarly with the question of conversion. While there are conflicting views within the tradition about proselytes, some very positive, some very negative, the rabbinic tradition never encouraged proselytization. For Halevi, converts could

only become the equals of native Jews after many generations of intermarriage between them. For certain strands of
the Midrash and for the *Zohar* conversion as such was really
not possible. Converts were actually persons of Gentile par-
entage into whom intrinsically Jewish souls happened to find
their way. Conversion, then was not really the issue, so much
as returning an errant soul to its proper place. Gentiles not
having such souls could never truly convert to Judaism.
Maimonides rejected these views altogether, welcomed
sincere proselytes wholeheartedly, allowed for proselytization, and adopted a warmly positive attitude toward the
whole issue of conversion. Given that we are at basis the
same, and given that one day all humans would convert to
Judaism, Maimonides had no reason to have reservations
about sincere proselytes, and may even have seen in the welcoming of proselytes an anticipation of the messianic era.
Yea or nay, Maimonides's views on this issue are a consequence of his philosophical psychology.

Maimonides's views on dogma are absolutely unprece-
dented in the Judaism that developed to his day. These views
are examined in chapter 7. The essence of being and becoming a Jew, and of earning a place in the world to come,
Maimonides teaches, involves the acceptance or rejection of
certain views. Defining a Jew in terms of the views which he
or she accepts goes hand in hand with a view of human
nature that insists that all humans are basically alike, distinguished, to the extent that they are distinguished, only by the
views they adopt. Thus Maimonides's philosophical psychology plays a role in one of his religiously most unusual claims,
that concerning the place and nature of dogma in Judaism.

What sort of views are those the adoption of which is
crucial for being Jewish? A discussion of that issue forms the
substance of chapter 8. These views turn out to be the science
of the Torah in its true sense which, in turn, is *ma'aseh bereshit*
and *ma'aseh merkavah*, physics and metaphysics. The body of
knowledge to be mastered, then, if one wishes to become a
Jew, or, if already a Jew, to become a perfected Jew, is difficult but not occult or esoteric. Any normally intelligent person can master it to one degree or another. One sees yet

again the footprints of Maimonides's nonessentialist definition of what a Jew is, which, in turn, is a consequence of his
philosophical psychology.

The last issue taken up in this study is the nature of *Klal
Yisrael*, the people of Israel. Maimonides distinguishes the
Jewish people, defined in terms of their descent from the
Patriarch Abraham, from "Israel," defined in terms of its
acceptance of the philosophical views taught in the true science of the Torah. Maimonides is consistent in all his writings, avoiding all essentialist definitions of Israel in favor of
the theory described here. Having adopted his philosophical
psychology, he could do no other.

The positions of Maimonides the philosopher and Rambam the rabbi form a seamless whole, each fructifying and
enriching the other.

Citations from Maimonides's Works

Notes

Chapter 1

1. See Jacob Katz, *Tradition and Crisis: Jewish Society at the End of the Middle Ages* (New York: Schocken, 1971), p. 26. Subsequent citations from Katz are drawn from this and the following page.

2. It is interesting and of some contemporary relevance to note how these views find expression in the modern world. See Arthur Hertzberg, *The Jews in America* (New York: Simon & Schuster, 1989), p. 329.

> When Jews were asked about their identity, it was possible for many of them to assert that their loyalty was to the Jewish people, and never mind faith in God. The sense of being one people, one family, as the seed of Abraham, had always been central in Jewish consciousness. This self–definition had become more pervasive in the 1950s, as American Jews increasingly identified with the new State of Israel. In Israel, all Jews belonged to the nation, even though many were indifferent to the Jewish religion.

Hertzberg (p. 387) finds such views disturbing.

> Such an assertion did not belong together with their usual rhetoric about ethnic pluralism. An ethnic group cannot

assert "chosenness" without falling into chauvinism or worse. In a democratic society, only a religion dare use this term and only to describe believers who are committed to live spiritual lives.

3. See, for example, *Phaedo,* 69Eff and *Meno,* 81A. See also W. K. C. Guthrie, "Plato's Views on the Nature of the Soul," *Entretiens sur l'antiquite classique,* 3. *Recherches sur la tradition Platonicienne* (Geneva: Vandoeuvres, 1955), pp. 3–19.

4. *De Anima,* II.1 (412aff.). For some of the necessary qualifications, see Arthur Hyman, "Aristotle's Theory of the Intellect and Its Interpretation by Averroes," in Dominic J. O'Meara (ed.), *Studies in Aristotle* (Washington: Catholic University of American Press, 1981): 161–91 (= *Studies in Philosophy and the History of Philososphy* 9).

5. As Maimonides says, "Through it ["the conception of intelligibles which teach true view concerning metaphysics"] man is man." I quote here from *The Guide of the Perplexed,* translated by Shlomo Pines (Chicago: University of Chicago Press, 1963). The passage just quoted is from *Guide* III.54, p. 635.

6. Judah Halevi, *Kuzari,* translated by Hartwig Hirschfeld (New York: Schocken, 1964), I.1, pp. 36–37. Further citations from Halevi will be from this translation. For the differences between this exposition and the longer one in *Kuzari,* V.12, see pp. 210–17 in Pines, "Shi'ite Terms and Conceptions in Judah Halevi's *Kuzari," Jerusalem Studies in Arabic and Islam* 2 (1980): 165–251.

7. See, for example, *Guide of the Perplexed,* III.27, p. 511.

8. See Warren Zev Harvey, "Rabbi Hasdai Crescas and His Critique of Philosophic Happiness," *Proceedings of the Sixth World Congress of Jewish Studies* 3 (Jerusalem: World Congress of Jewish Studies, 1977): 143–49 (Hebrew).

9. See p. 139 in Majid Fakhry, "The Contemplative Ideal in Islamic Philosophy: Aristotle and Avicenna," *Journal of the History of Philosophy* 14 (1976): 137–45.

The whole process of human cognition thus becomes a gradual progression or ascent from the lowest condition of potentiality to the highest condition of actuality, or the apprehension of those intelligibles stored away in the active intellect. The name that Ibn Sina and his successors gave to this progression is not union with, or even vision of, but rather conjunction or contact (*ittisal*) with the active intellect.

For the theory of the acquired intellect in ibn Sina and al–Farabi, see Herbert Davidson's important study, "Alfrabi and Avicenna on the Active Intellect," *Viator* 3 (1972): 109–78; for our purposes here, the relevant passages are 137–44 (al–Farabi) and 160–68 (ibn Sina). The question of the nature of the contact with the Active Intellect became crucial in medieval Muslim and Jewish philosophy but need not detain us here. The bibliography on medieval Muslim and Jewish philosophical psychology is literally enormous. Studies that may be consulted include Fazlur Rahman, *Avicenna's Psychology* (London: Geoffrey Cumberlege for Oxford University Press, 1952); Warren Harvey, "Hasdai Crescas's Critique of the Theory of the Acquired Intellect," Ph.D. diss., Columbia University, 1973, p. 28, note 1; Seymour Feldman's introduction to his translation of Gersonides's *Wars of the Lord,* I (Philadelphia: Jewish Publication Society, 1984), pp. 71–84); and Feldman, "Gersonides on the Possiblity of Conjunction with the Agent Intellect," *AJS Review* 3 (1978): 99–120. All of these studies contain references to the relevant scholarly literature.

10. Maimonides's notorious intellectual elitism is an expression of this. See, for example, "Laws of the Foundations of the Torah," IV.11; *Guide of the Perplexed,* I, Introduction, p. 16; and especially the text from *Guide,* III.18, p. 475 discussed in chapter 4, p. 24. It is interesting to note that in addition to being used to justify intellectual elitism, this Aristotelian theory has also been used to argue against the possibility of the transmigration of souls. See Aviezer Ravitzky, "'The Feet of the Kabbalists Stand Upon the Heads of the Philosophers'?—On the Disputation in Candia in the Fifteenth Century," *Tarbiz* 58 (1990): 453–82, pp. 575f.

11. For an argument to the effect that Sa'adia's position is close to Plato's, see Herbert A. Davidson, "Sa'adia's List of Theories of the Soul," in A. Altmann (ed.), *Jewish Medieval and Renaissance Studies* (Cambridge: Harvard University Press, 1967): 75–94, p. 87. See Davidson's notes for further studies on Sa'adia's theory of the soul.

12. Sa'adia Gaon, *Book of Beliefs and Opinions,* VI.3, translated by Samuel Rosenblatt (New Haven: Yale University Press, 1948), p. 241.

13. See Ephraim E. Urbach, *Hazal* (Jerusalem: Magnes, 1969), pp. 208–20.

14. Niddah, 30b.

15. *Kuzari,* I.1 and V.12; On Avicenna's reading of Aristotle, see Rahman (above, note 9), pp. 3–19. For an interpretation of Halevi's relationship to his philosophical sources, see Yohanan Silman, *Bein Philosoph li–Navi* (Ramat Gan, Israel: Bar Ilan University Press, 1985).

16. On this special characteristic, the *inyan elohi* (Arabic: *al–amr al–ilahi*) in Halevi, see Harry A. Wolfson, "Hallevi and Maimonides on Prophecy," *JQR* 32 (1942): 345–70 and 33 (1942): 49–82, reprinted in Wolfson, *Studies in the History of Philosophy and Religion,* II (Cambridge: Harvard University Press, 1977): 60–119. For an interpretation of Halevi's view of the Jewish people, see Yohanan Silman, "The Systematic Reasons for the Idea of the Election of Israel in the *Kuzari,*" *Sinai* 80 (1977): 253–64 (Hebrew). Representative texts from the *Kuzari* on this issue include the following: "But the Law was given to us because He led us out of Egypt, and remained attached to us, because we are the pick of mankind" (I.27, p. 47); "Therefore you [the Jews] rank above all the other inhabitants of the earth" (I.96, p. 67); "The sons of Jacob were, however, distinguished from other people by godly qualities, which made them, so to speak, an angelic caste" (I.103, p. 73); "Israel amidst the nations is like the heart among the organs of the body" (II.36, p. 109); "Thou knowest that the elements gradually evolved metals, plants, animals, man, finally the pure of essence of man [i.e., the Jewish people]. The whole evolution took place for the sake of this essence, in order that the *inyan elohi* should inhabit it" (II.44, p. 110); see further II.50 (p. 114); III.1 (p. 136); III.17 (p. 152); and IV.3 (p. 207). Fairness to Halevi demands that we take note of the special circumstances surrounding the adoption of his position, and that we not accuse him of nor blame him for twentieth century racism. Halevi flourished in a place and time in which conflicting national and religious groupings each advanced its own claims to nobility and belittled the character of its opponents. Christian Spaniards affirmed their superiority over Jews and Muslims; Muslims affirmed their superiority over Jews and Christians; Muslim Arabs affirmed their superiority over non–Arab Muslims; Halevi affirmed the superiority of the Jews over the Spaniards, Arabs, and North Africans.

17. Gershom Scholem, *Major Trends in Jewish Mysticism* (New York: Schocken, 1941), pp. 241–42.

18. I use this term for the sake of convenience; I do not mean to assert (or deny) that philosophical views influenced the Rabbis or that Sa'adia, Halevi, or the *Zohar* derived their views from Plato and not from rabbinic sources.

19. The *Zohar* teaches that Jewish souls originate in holiness while those of Gentiles originate in the *sitra ahra* (satanic forces). See, for example, *Zohar*, part III, p. 25b. For a very useful analysis of these issues, and for a nuanced exposition of Kabbalistic views on the nature of Gentiles, see Moshe Hallamish, "Some Aspects of the Attitudes of the Kabbalists Towards Gentiles," in Asa Kasher and Moshe Hallamish (eds.), *Philosophiah Yisraelit* (Tel Aviv: Papyrus [University of Tel Aviv]: 1983): 49–71 (Hebrew). On the issue of the holy origin of Jewish souls versus the impure origin of Gentile souls, see Hallamish, p. 53.

20. See *Kuzari*, I.27 (p. 47: "Any Gentile who joins us unconditionally shares our good fortune, without, however, being quite equal to us") and I.115 (p. 79: "Those, however, who become Jews do not take equal rank with born Israelites, who are specially privileged to attain prophecy, whilst the former can only achieve something by learning from them, and can only become pious and learned, but never prophets.")

21. Lasker's metaphor may be found in "Proselyte Judaism, Christianity, and Islam in the Thought of Judah Halevi," *JQR* 81 (1990), forthcoming. My use of the expression, "native Jew," is based on Lasker's locution, "native–born Jew." Professor Lasker was kind enough to allow me to see a prepublication copy of his fine study and I am pleased to express my thanks to him.

22. For a summary and analysis of Zoharic statements to this effect, see Jochanan H. A. Wijnhoven, "The Zohar and the Proselyte," in Michael A. Fishbane and Paul R. Flohr (eds.), *Texts and Responses: Studies Presented to Nahum N. Glatzer . . .* (Leiden: Brill, 1975): 120–40.

23. See *Zohar*, part III, p. 168a and part II, pp. 95b and 98b, translated into Hebrew with commentary in I. Tishbi, *Mishnat ha–Zohar*, I, 3d. ed. (Jerusalem: Mossad Bialik, 1971), pp. 50 and 62–64. For rabbinic sources of this idea, see *Numbers Rabbah* XIII.15–16 and Shevuot 39a.

24. For other but related Kabbalistic positions on these questions, see Hallamish, "Attitudes of Kabbalists," pp. 56–57.

25. See Pines, "Translator's Introduction," in his translation of
Maimonides's *Guide of the Perplexed* (Chicago: University of Chicago
Press, 1963), p. cxvii; and my discussion of his position in *Maimonides on Human Perfection* (Atlanta: Scholar Press, 1990).

26. Pines, Foreward to David Hartman, *Maimonides: Torah and
Philosophic Quest* (Philadelphia: Jewish Publication Society, 1976), p.
xi. It is a mark of Pines's greatness that the book to which he wrote
this foreward is devoted to refuting his interpretation of Maimonides. For a masterful exposition of Pines's views and their underlying assumptions, see W. Zev Harvey, "On Professor Shlomo Pines
and his Approach to Jewish Thought," in *Sefer ha–Yovel li–Shlomo
Pines . . .* I (= *Jerusalem Studies in Jewish Thought* 7) (Jerusalem,
1988): 1–15 (Hebrew).

27. For further startling Pinesian claims about Maimonides see
my *Maimonides on Human Perfection*, p. 73.

Chapter 2

1. I am not one of those who attaches much importance to the
question of whether or not the *Guide* is a "philosophical" book.
Those who are interested in the question may want to consult
Joseph Buijs, "The Philosophical Character of Maimonides's
Guide— A Critique of Strauss' Interpretation," *Judaism* 27 (1978):
448–57. A valuable summary and analysis of approaches to this
issue may be found in Arthur Hyman, "Interpreting Maimonides,"
Gesher 5 (1976): 46–59. Both essays are now available in Joseph A.
Buijs (ed.), *Maimonides: A Collection of Critical Essays* (Notre Dame:
University of Notre Dame Press, 1988).

2. Arabic: *al–'ilm al–ilahi*; Ibn Tibbon: *he–hokhmah ha–elohit*.
By this Maimonides means "metaphysics." See his statements to this
effect in his commentary to Mishnah Hagigah II.1 (in the complete
edition of R. Joseph Kafih, *Mishnah im Perush Rabbenu Moshe ben
Maimon* [Jerusalem: Mossad ha–Rav Kook, 1963], 2, p. 377)
(henceforth, "Kafih") and the discussion in M. Kellner, "The Conception of Torah as a Deductive Science in Medieval Jewish
Thought," *REJ* 146 (1987): 265–79. See further, Maimonides's *Art
of Logic*, chapter 14, and my discussion in chapter 8, pp. 65–69.

3. *Guide*, II.2 (p. 253); compare *Guide*, II, Introduction, p. 239.
See also *Guide*, I, Introduction, pp. 6–7 for an account of why

Maimonides did write the book. In a letter to Samuel ibn Tibbon Maimonides reiterates his disavowal of any intention to write a comprehensive philosophical text or a work for beginners in philosophy. See Yaakov Shilat (ed.), *Iggerot ha–Rambam* (Jerusalem: Ma'aliyot, 1988), vol. 2, p. 545 (henceforth, "Shilat").

4. *Guide*, I.68, p. 126. Compare Alexander Altmann, "Maimonides on the Intellect and the Scope of Metaphysics," in Altmann's *Von der mittelalterlichen zur modernen Aufklaerung* (Tuebingen: Mohr, 1987): 60–129, p. 60: "Nowhere in his writings does Maimonides offer a systematic account of the intellect, notwithstanding the fact that the topic is of central significance in his thinking." Altmann's posthumously published essay supplies the lack, offering a systematic account of Maimonides's theory of the intellect. Interestingly, in another chapter Maimonides writes: "Do not criticize the terms applied to the intellect in this chapter and others. For the purpose here is to guide towards the intended notion and not to investigate the truth of the essence of the intellect; for other chapters are devoted to a precise account of this subject" (I.32, p. 70). Maimonides's commentators, both medieval and modern, see here a reference to I.68 and I.72. There is no contradiction: an account of intellect as such is not a full account of the soul.

5. Two recent and valuable studies supply this want to a considerable extent. Altmann, "Maimonides on the Intellect" collects and analyzes Maimonides's statements on the intellect. Barry Kogan, "'What Can We Know and When Can We Know It?' Maimonides on the Active Intelligence and Human Cognition," in Eric L. Ormsby (ed.), *Moses Maimonides and His Time* (= *Studies in Philosophy and the History of Philosophy* 19) (Washington: Catholic University of America Press, 1989), pp. 121–37, analyzes Maimonides's statements on the intellect in the light of the discussions of ibn Sina, Al–Farabi, and ibn Bajja with an eye toward showing which of the three Maimonides most closely resembles (Kogan shows that Maimonides's epistemology is closest to that of ibn Sina). Both of these important essays, however, assume that Maimonides does in fact adopt some variant of the theory of the acquired intellect, and neither focuses precisely on the issue on which I wish to concentrate here. A further useful study relevant to our theme is Howard Kreisel, "Maimonides on the Practical Intellect, *HUCA* 69 (1988): 189–215. In addition to Crescas, who both attributes the theory to Maimonides and criticizes him for it (see W. Z. Harvey's article and dissertation, cited in chapter 1, notes 8 and 9), another

medieval thinker who attributed it to Maimonides was Profiat Duran. See Dov Rappel, "Profiat Duran's Introduction to *Sefer Ma'aseh Efod*," Yizhak Raphael (ed.), *Sinai Centenary Volume* (Jerusalem: Mossad ha–Rav Kook, 1987), Vol. II: 749–95, p. 770 (Hebrew).

6. I refer to the approaches of Lawrence V. Berman and Shlomo Pines. See chapter 1, notes 25 and 26, and my book, *Maimonides on Human Perfection*. Oliver Leaman's new study, *Moses Maimonides* (London: Routledge, 1990), should be noted in this regard as well. The book appeared in a series called "Arabic Thought and Culture" but, withal, rejects the esoteric approach of Pines and Berman.

7. It is primarily to this idea that I refer when I assert that Maimonides adopted some variant of the theory of the acquired intellect. I keep saying "some variant" because it is not my purpose here to inquire into the question of Maimonides's historical sources (on that, see the excellent studies by Altmann, Kogan, and Kreisel), important as that question is, nor is it my purpose to inquire into the nature of the conjunction or lack thereof with the Active Intellect or God by virtue of which we acquire intellect, nor is it my purpose to inquire into the question of what precise sort of intellectual apprehensions are necessary in order to acquire intellect (on which see Harvey's "R. Hasdai Crescas and his Critique."), nor, finally, is it my intention to inquire directly into the question of whether or not intellectual apprehensions of some sort afford us immortality of some sort; rather, it is sufficient for me to show that according to Maimonides all human beings are, exceptional aptitudes or deficiencies aside, born with a roughly equivalent potential to apprehend intelligibles, thereby actualizing their intellects, and thereby achieving one level or other of human perfection.

8. I quote from the text as translated in R. L. Weiss and C. Butterworth, *Ethical Writings of Maimonides* (New York: Dover, 1983), p. 64. Further on the intellect, see also *Guide* I.73 (p. 209).

9. See *Guide*, III.8.

10. Weiss and Butterworth, *Writings of Maimonides*, p. 65.

11. Herbert A. Davidson, "Maimonides' *Shemonah Peraqim* and Alfarabi's *Fusul al–Madani*," *PAAJR* 31 (1963): 33–50 proves Maimonides's extensive use of Al–Farabi in the composition of the "Eight Chapters." Our text is based on *Fusul al–Madani*, section 7. See Davidson, p. 38, note 16.

12. Kafih, *Mishnah*, IV, p. 205.

13. Following Kogan, "What Can We Know?" it is reasonable to assume that Maimonides has ibn Sina in mind here. As we saw in chapter 1, note 9, this is indeed ibn Sina's position.

14. I quote from the translation of Moses Hyamson, *The Book of Knowledge* (New York: Feldheim, 1974), p. 39a.

15. "Laws of Repentance," VIII.3 (Hyamson, pp. 90a–b) (emphasis added). This whole chapter is relevant to our theme.

16. By "overflow" (i.e., "emanation;" Hebrew, *shefa*; Arabic, *fayd*) Maimonides means the activity peculiar to a being separate from matter. See *Guide*, II.12 (p. 274). Maimonides's statement here does not mean that the acquired intellect exists independently of and antecedently to our intellectual activities. We acquire, in effect create, our acquired intellects. Once acquired, they do indeed affect our behavior and thus "overflow towards" us. Compare Altmann, "Maimonides on the Intellect," pp. 75–80.

17. This view should not be confused with that of Plato or with Sa'adia's variant of the Platonic view. According to Plato and Sa'adia we are equipped with fully formed souls when we are born; according to Maimonides we have a potential to become intellects.

18. On this last point, compare *Guide*, I.1.

Chapter 3

1. "*Hilkhot De'ot*" has been translated in many ways. Maimonides himself, however, in *Guide*, III.35 (p. 535) tells us that this section of the *Mishneh Torah* deals with "the improvement of *al–akhlaq*." I follow Pines in translating *al–akhlaq* as "moral qualities." Here is the passage in full: "The third class comprises the *commandments* concerning with improvement of the moral qualities. They are those that we have enumerated in *Hilkhot De'ot*." Curiously, Pines here translates *Hilkhot De'ot* as "Laws Concerning Opinions," perhaps the least likely of all the translations I have seen.

2. Maimonides's *Makalah fi–Sina'at al–Mantik* is the first of his known works. It was translated into Hebrew three times in the Middle Ages. Those portions of the Arabic text then known and the three Hebrew translations were edited and published by Israel

Efros under the title, *Maimonides' Treatise on Logic* (New York: American Academy for Jewish Research, 1938). This comprised all of volume X of the *Proceedings of the American Academy for Jewish Research*. The entire Arabic text was discovered in Turkey and published there twice in 1960 by Mubahat Turker. Efros then published the complete text (in Hebrew letters) in *PAAJR* 34 (1966): 155–60 (English) and 9–42 (Hebrew). For further details (including data on Turker's editions), see Lawrence V. Berman, "Some Remarks on the Arabic Text of Maimonides' 'Treatise on the Art of Logic'," *JAOS* 88 (1968): 340–42; and Israel Efros, "Maimonides' Treatise on Logic: The New Arabic Text and its Light on the Hebrew Versions," *JQR* 53 (1962–63): 267–73. On chapter XIV in particular, see Harry Austryn Wolfson, "The Classification of the Sciences in Medieval Jewish Philosophy," in his *Studies in the History of Philosophy and Religion*, I (Cambridge: Harvard University Press, 1973): 493–545 (from which source it will be quoted later); Leo Strauss, "Maimonides' Statement on Political Science," *PAAJR* 22 (1953): 115–30; and Lawrence V. Berman, "A Re–Examination of Maimonides' Statement on Political Science," *JAOS* 89 (1969): 106–11. For a recent study on the *Art of Logic* see Raymond L. Weiss, "On the Scope of Maimonides' *Logic*, Or, What Joseph Knew," in R. Link–Salinger (ed.), *A Straight Path: Studies in Medieval Philosophy and Culture, Essays in Honor of Arthur Hyman* (Washington, D.C.: Catholic University of America Press, 1988): 255–65.

3. Arabic: *al–akhlaq*.

4. Arabic: *al–hay'at al–mushtamila*.

5. Arabic: *fada'il*.

6. Wolfson, pp. 538–39.

7. Maimonides's "Eight Chapters" is the name popularly given to his introduction to his commentary on the mishnaic tractate Avot. For the Arabic text and a modern Hebrew translation see Kafih, *Mishnah*, IV.

8. I quote here and later from the translation found in Weiss and Butterworth (eds.), *Ethical Writings of Maimonides*, 61.

9. Weiss and Butterworth, pp. 60–61; emphasis added. With respect to Maimonides's comment in this passage, "hear the truth from whoever says it," reference should be made to two further passages in his writings where a similar idea finds expression. In *Guide*, III.8 (p. 267) Maimonides states that the Sages, unlike Aris-

totle, erred in claiming that the movement of the spheres made sounds. He explains that there is nothing wrong with attributing error to the Sages in these matters: "[The Sages themselves] in these astronomical matters preferred the opinion of the sages of the nations of the world to their own. For the explicitly say, 'The Sages of the world have vanquished' [Pesahim 94b]. And this is correct. For everyone who argues in speculative matters does this according to the conclusions to which he was led by his speculation. Hence the conclusion whose demonstration is correct is believed." The truth is what counts, not the identity of the person who said it. We find a similar idea in the *Mishneh Torah*, "Laws of the Sanctification of the New Moon" XVII.24: "In that all these matters are established with clear proofs that are beyond reproach, such that one cannot possibly doubt them, we do not concern ourselves with their authors, whether they were composed by prophets or by gentile authors. For with respect to everything the reason of which has been discovered, and the truth of which has been made known through proofs that are beyond reproach, we rely upon he who said it . . ."

10. Maimonides appeals to the authority of the Rabbis, then, in support of his positions. To the extent that the interpretations of Maimonides put forward in this book are correct, it seems that Maimonides would want to say that the positions herein attributed to him are not only his positions, but those of the Rabbis as well. On Maimonides's claim that the Rabbis taught philosophy, see my discussion of *Guide*, II.11 in chapter 8 (p. 93) and my *Dogma in Medieval Jewish Thought* (Oxford: Oxford University Press, 1986), p. 234 (note 169) and my *Maimonides on Human Perfection*, p. 80 (note 72).

11. See Davidson, "Maimonides' *Shemonah Peraqim*."

12. See Raymond L. Weiss, "The Adaptation of Philosophic Ethics to a Religious Community: Maimonides's *Eight Chapters*," *PAAJR* 54 (1987): 261–87.

13. And, of course, from Aristotle as well. For Maimonides's use of Aristotle in his ethics, see Marvin Fox, "The Doctrine of the Mean in Aristotle and Maimonides: A Comparative Study," in S. Stein and R. Loewe (eds.), *Studies in Jewish Religious and Intellectual History Presented to Alexander Altmann* (University [Alabama]: University of Alabama Press, 1979): 93–120; Daniel H. Frank, "Humility as a Virtue: A Maimonidean Critique of Aristotle's Ethics," in

Eric L. Ormsby (ed.), *Moses Maimonides and His Time* (Washington: Catholic University of America Press, 1989): 89–99 (= *Studies in Philosophy and the History of Philosophy* 19), and; importantly, Steven Schwarzschild, "Moral Radicalism and 'Middlingness' in the Ethics of Maimonides," *Studies in Medieval Culture* 11 (1978): 65–94 (reprinted in M. Kellner [ed.], *The Pursuit of the Ideal: Jewish Writings of Steven Schwarzschild* [Albany: SUNY Press, 1990]: 137–60).

14. Weiss and Butterworth, *Maimonides,* p. 68; emphasis added.

15. Weiss and Butterworth, *Maimonides,* pp. 83–84. Maimonides goes on here to point out that "it is possible to be naturally disposed towards a virtue or a vice" but that such inclinations can be overcome by training. There is a text in the *Guide,* that might be thought to contradict Maimonides's claim here no one is born possessing virtues or vices. In II.30 (p. 357) Maimonides emphasizes the following passage from Tractate Shabbat 146a: "When the serpent came to Eve, it cast pollution into her. The pollution of [the sons of] Israel, who had been present at Mt. Sinai, has come to an end. [As for] the nations who were not present at Mt. Sinai, their pollution has not come to an end." On the face of it, this would seem to indicate that Jews are born purer than non–Jews. The proper reading of this text would seem to be, however, that, having been subverted by imagination, human beings became subject to their physical appetites. The Jews, thanks to the Torah, are able to overcome their appetites and achieve moral perfection. This is much harder for non–Jews, who do not have the Torah. Maimonides's medieval and modern commentators are unanimous in so reading him. On this, see my book, *Maimonides on Human Perfection,* pp. 76–77 (note 47).

16. Weiss and Butterworth, *Maimonides,* p. 84; emphasis added.

17. Hebrew: *le–khol ehad ve–ehad mibnai adam.*

18. Weiss and Butterworth, *Maimonides,* p. 28. On "Laws of Moral Qualities" specifically, see Raymond L. Weiss, "Law and Ethics: Reflections on Maimonides 'Ethics'," *Journal of the History of Philosophy* 9 (1971): 425–33.

19. For differences between the discussions, see Herbert A. Davidson, "The Middle Way in Maimonides' Ethics," *PAAJR* 54 1987): 31–72.

20. *De'ot*; Weiss and Butterworth have "character traits."

21. "Laws of Moral Qualities," I.7. Weiss and Butterworth, *Maimonides*, p. 30.

22. Weiss and Butterworth, *Maimonides*, p. 31. Compare "Eight Chapters," fourth chapter, Weiss and Butterworth, *Maimonides*, pp. 68–69.

Chapter 4

1. In a number of places Maimonides clearly defines "human perfection" in terms of intellectual perfection. See, for example, "Laws of Moral Qualities," III.2, "Laws of Tefilin," VI.13, *Guide of the Perplexed*, I.2 (p. 24), I.30, III.8 (p. 432), III.27 (p. 511), III.28 (p. 512), III.51 (pp. 621 and 627–28) and III.54 (p. 635) and the discussion in my book, *Maimonides on Human Perfection*, pp. 1–5. I should like to point out here that the point of this last–mentioned monograph is to prove that for Maimonides human perfection means intellectual perfection; the perfection available to and demanded of those Jews capable of it, however, is higher. The perfected Jew imitates God, after reaching the heights of intellectual perfection, through a species of practical work in this world: obedience to the commandments of the Torah properly understood.

2. As we have seen, Maimonides said, "Through it, man is man" (III.54, p. 635). See also Maimonides's commentary to Mishnah Bava Kama IV.3 where Maimonides says that one whose human characteristics have not been actualized is not truly a human being; such a one exists only to serve the perfected human being. See further *Guide*, I.7 (pp. 32–33): "You know that whoever is not endowed with this form [i.e., intellect], whose signification we have explained, is not a man, but an animal having the shape and configuration of a man."

3. Important studies of Maimonides's views on providence include Zvi Diesendruck, "Samuel and Moses ibn Tibbon on Maimonides' Theory of Providence," *HUCA* 11 (1936): 341–66; and Avraham Nuriel, "Providence and Guidance in the *Guide of the Perplexed*," *Tarbiz* 49 (1980): 346–55 (Hebrew).

4. Maimonides's position may be profitably contrasted with that of Hasdai Crescas. In his *Light of the Lord* Crescas explicitly affirms that God extends special providence to the Jews as a group.

The claim is made in Treatise II ("On Prophecy"), part ii, chapter 1 (p. 35a in the Vienna, 1859 edition) and explained in II.ii.6 (pp. 38b–39b). For light on Crescas's latter discussion, see Daniel J. Lasker, "Original Sin and its Atonement According to Hasdai Crescas," *Da'at* 20 (1988): 127–35 (Hebrew). Other medieval Jewish philosophers who held similar views include Abraham Bibago and Abraham Shalom. For Bibago, see *Path of Faith* (*Derekh Emunah*), treatise I, part iii (Constantinople, 1522 [photoreproduction, Jerusalem: Mekorot, 1970], p. 18a) and III.v (p. 99d) and Allan Lazaroff, *The Theology of Abraham Bibago* (University: University of Alabama Press, 1981), p. 46. For Abraham Shalom, see *Abode of Peace* (*Neveh Shalom*), treatise IV, chapter 1 (Venice, 1575; photoreproduction: Westmead [England]: Gregg International, 1969, p. 54a), II.9 (pp. 37a–b), IV.2 (p. 54a), IX.1 (p. 153a) and X.3 (p. 176b), and Herbert A. Davidson, *The Philosophy of Abraham Shalom* (Berkeley: University of California Press, 1964), pp. 73–75. Isaac Abravanel, in terms apparently influenced by Halevi's essentialist definition of the nature of the Jewish people, also insisted that Israel enjoyed a providential care not extended to other nations. See his commentary to Gen. 11:1, his introduction to his commentary on Exod., and his commentary on Exod. 23:20. See further, *Crown of the Elders* (*Ateret Zekenim*) chapters 12 and 14 (Warsaw, 1894, pp. 37–38 and 50–51). Even Gersonides, who generally takes more radically Aristotelian positions than Maimonides, allows for special providence (in his very Maimonidean sense of providence) for the people of Israel. See his *Wars of the Lord*, treatise II, chapter 6 (in the translation of Seymour Feldman, *The Wars of the Lord*, 2 [Philadelphia: Jewish Publication Society, 1987], pp. 199ff). On Gersonides on providence see J. David Bleich, *Providence in the Philosophy of Gersonides* (New York: Yeshiva University Press, 1973) and my article, "Gersonides, Providence, and the Rabbinic Tradition," *JAAR* 42 (1974): 673–85.

5. P. 469; emphasis and material in brackets added.

6. P. 471; emphasis added.

7. Pines has "overflow."

8. Maimonides's use of Arabic names in this context is not only a function of the fact that the *Guide* was written in Arabic, but a reflection of his rejection of the claim that providence is unique to or more emphatically found among the Jews than among human beings generally.

9. See Maimonides's statements in his "Epistle to Yemen." "Our disbelief in the prophecies of Omar and Zeid is not due to the fact that they are non–Jews, as the unlettered folk imagine." And "Now, if a Jewish or gentile prophet urges and encourages people to follow the religion of Moses without adding thereto or diminishing therefrom." I quote from the translation of A. S. Halkin in *Crisis and Leadership: Epistles of Maimonides* (Philadelphia: Jewish Publication Society, 1985), pp. 111 and 113. For the Arabic text and three medieval Hebrew translations see A. S. Halkin (ed.) *Moses Maimonides' Epistle to Yemen* (New York: American Academy for Jewish Research, 1952), pp. 56ff. For the Arabic text and a modern Hebrew translation see Rabbi J. Kafih (ed.), *Iggerot ha–Rambam* (Jerusalem: Mossad ha–Rav Kook, 1972), pp. 36 and 38. See also the helpful analysis in Ya'akov Levinger, "Human Perfection among the Gentiles According to Maimonides," *Hagut* II: *Bein Yisrael li–Amim* (Jerusalem: Ministry of Education and Culture, 1978): 27–36 (Hebrew). Levinger republished this (and many other of his articles) in his book, *Ha–Rambam ki–Philosoph u–ki–Posek* (Jerusalem: Mossad Bialik, 1989); the article there appears under the title, "Prophecy as a General Human Phenomenon" (pp. 21–28). Levinger comments that Maimonides was the first and perhaps only medieval Jewish philosopher to see prophecy as a general human possibility, and not something unique to Israel. See further, Norbert M. Samuelson, "Ibn Daud's Conception of Prophecy, *Journal of the American Academy of Religion* 45 (1977) (Supplement): 883–900.

10. See *Guide*, II.32–38. Note well that Maimonides opens his discussion of prophecy in "Laws of the Foundations of the Torah," VII thusly, "It is among the foundations of religion [*dat*] to know that God causes *human beings* [*bnei ha-adam*] to prophesy" (emphasis added). In no place in this *halakhic* text does Maimonides qualify this claim, restricting prophecy to Jews.

11. I should note that on my view Maimonides posits the *theoretical* possibility that non–Jews can prophesy. But, given that intellectual perfection is a necessary prerequisite for prophecy, and given that moral perfection is a necessary condition for intellectual perfection, and that obedience to Torah is close to being a necessary condition for moral perfection (See *Guide*, II.30 and the discussion in my book, *Maimonides on Human Perfection*, pp. 28–31), Maimonides would be very surprised to find any non–Jews *actually* prophesying.

12. Maimonides is aware of the fact that some individuals are born with limited intellectual capabilities; he is interested here, as everywhere, in the rule, and not in exceptions to the rule. On this last, see *Guide*, III.12 (p. 448). Maimonides is also aware of the fact that some individuals are born with exceptional aptitudes (see his comments in *Guide*, II.32, p. 362 on Jer. 1:5–6) and that individuals are born predisposed to develop different moral qualities (see chapter 3, p. 20). But, as above, it is the general rule that is crucial and all normal human beings are born with a roughly equal capacity for intellectual perfection.

13. See *Kuzari*, I.99, I.115, II.10–14, II.67, III.1, and IV. 10. See further, Yohanan Silman, *Bein Philosoph li–Navi*, pp. 135, 140, 146, and 158.

14. See his *Exalted Faith*, part I, Basic Principle v, chapter 1. See the translation of Norbert M. Samuelson, *The Exalted Faith by Abraham ibn Daud* (Rutherford, N.J.: Farleigh Dickinson University Press and London: Associated University Presses, 1986), pp. 195–96 and commentary, p. 199. On Halevi and ibn Daud see also Samuelson's "Ibn Daud's Conception of Prophecy."

15. See Albo's *Book of Principles* (*Sefer ha–Ikkarim*), treatise III, chapter 11. I quote from the translation of Isaac Husik, *Sefer ha–Ikkarim* (Philadelphia: Jewish Publication Society, 1946), vol. 3, p. 104.

16. See Abravanel's commentary to *Guide*, II.32. I quote from the translation of Alvin Reines in *Maimonides and Abrabanel on Prophecy* (Cincinnati: Hebrew Union College Press, 1970), p. 24.

17. Hebrew: *bnai ha–adam.*

18. Hebrew: *yezer.*

19. Hebrew: *da'ato.*

20. As opposed to one whose temperament is still "effervescent." See *Guide*, III.51, p. 627.

21. Hebrew: *de'ah.*

22. II.32–48. I cannot forbear pointing out that the numbers 32 and 48, when written in Hebrew letters, spell out the words *heart* and *brain* (*lev* and *mo'ah*). Perhaps I have opened a whole new area of research here, beyond Straussian numerology, into Maimonidean gematriah!

23. P. 361; emphasis added.

24. Although, as just noted, Maimonides did not expect the world to be overrun by Gentile prophets since he held that without the Torah achieving the requisite moral perfection is well–nigh impossible.

25. "Laws of Kings," XII.2. I quote from the translation of A. M. Hershman, *The Book of Judges* (New Haven: Yale University Press, 1949), p. 241.

26. R. Eliezer's point appears to be that wicked Israelites and all Gentiles go to the nether world [Sheol].

27. Tosefta Sanhedrin, XIII.2. I quote, with emendations, from the translation in C. G. Montefiore and H. Loewe, *A Rabbinic Anthology* (New York: Schocken, 1974), p. 604.

28. Compare Ephraim E. Urbach, *Hazal* (Jerusalem: Magnes, 1969), pp. 480–94, esp. p. 482.

29. The question of how one defines a righteous Gentile, of course, becomes crucial. Maimonides's views will be presented below. See chapter 8, p. 75.

30. Kafih, IV, p. 205.

31. See chapter 2, page 12.

32. For a compilation and discussion of texts in the *Guide* bearing on immortality, see Altmann's "Maimonides on the Intellect," pp. 85–86.

33. P. 635; emphasis added.

34. For a contrary view, see Crescas's *Light of the Lord*, II.ii,6 (p. 38b).

Chapter 5

1. See Joseph Klausner, *The Messianic Idea in Israel* (New York: Macmillan, 1955).

2. I quote from the text as brought in Eliezer Ashkenazi, *Ta'am Zekenim* (Frankfurt, 1854), p. 60. For other places in which Rav Hai's responsum concerning salvation is preserved, see Zvi Groner, *A List of Hai Gaon's Responsa* [= *Alei Sefer* 13 (1986)] (Ramat Gan,

Israel, Bar Ilan University Press, 1968), p. 77 (no. 1097). For further information on the responsum see Yehudah Even–Shmuel, *Midrashei Ge'ulah* (Tel Aviv: Mossad Bialik/Massada, 1943), p. 134.

3. Maimonides's other discussions of messianism may be found in his introduction to the tenth chapter of Mishnah Sanhedrin ("Perek Helek") in his *Commentary on the Mishnah*, in "Laws of Repentance," IX, and in his "Epistle to Yemen." Of the studies of Maimonides's messianic doctrines relevant to our theme, the one that I have made the most use of is by my late and sorely lamented teacher and friend, Steven S. Schwarzschild. See his article, "A Note on the Nature of Ideal Society—A Rabbinic Study," in Strauss and Reissner (eds.), *Jubilee Volume Dedicated to Curt C. Silberman* (New York: Association of Jews from Central Europe, 1969): 86–15, reprinted in M. Kellner (ed.), *The Pursuit of the Ideal: Jewish Writings of Steven Schwarzschild* (Albany: SUNY Press, 1990): 99–108; other valuable studies include Amos Funkenstein, "Maimonides: Political Theory and Realistic Messianism," *Miscellanea Mediaevalia* 9 (1977): 81–103; Funkenstein, *Teva, Historiah, u–Meshihiut ezel ha–Rambam* (Tel Aviv: Ministry of Defense, 1983); David Hartman, "Sinai and Messianism," in his book, *Joy and Responsibility* (Jerusalem: Posner, 1983): 232–58; Hartman in A. S. Halkin (trans.), *Crisis and Leadership: Epistles of Maimonides* (Philadelphia: Jewish Publication Society, 1985): 150–207; Aviezer Ravitzky, "According to Human Capacity—The Messianic Era in the Teaching of Maimonides," in Z. Baras (ed.), *Meshihiut vi–Eschatalogiah* (Jerusalem: Merkaz Shazar, 1983): 191–220 (Hebrew), and Gershom Scholem, "Towards an Understanding of the Messianic Idea in Judaism," in *The Messianic Idea in Judaism* (New York: Schocken, 1971): 1–36; For our purposes in particular, Ya'akov Blidstein's study, *Ekronot Medini'im bi–Mishnat ha–Rambam* (Ramat Gan, Israel, Bar Ilan University Press, 1983): 227–33 is very important. I have examined some of the issues to be discussed here in "Messianic Postures in Israel Today," *Modern Judaism* 6 (1986): 197–209; and in "A Suggestion Concerning Maimonides' 'Thirteen Principles' and the Status of Non–Jews in the Messianic Era," in Meir Ayali (ed.), *Tura—Oranim Studies in Jewish Thought: Simon Greenberg Jubilee Volume* (Tel Aviv: Ha–Kibbutz ha–Meuhad, 1986): 249–60 (Hebrew). A few paragraphs of this chapter are drawn (in translation) from that article, and from my book, *Dogma in Medieval Jewish Thought*.

4. On this subject see Julius Greenstone, *The Messiah Idea in Jewish History* (Philadelphia: Jewish Publication Society, 1906);

Joseph Sarachek, *The Doctrine of the Messiah in Medieval Jewish Literature* (New York: Hermon Press, 1968); and Abba Hillel Silver, *A History of Messianic Speculation in Israel* (New York: Macmillan, 1927).

5. "Laws of Kings," XI.4. The text here is not without its problems, none of which, however, impinge upon our discussion. See Ya'akov Blidstein, "On Universal Rule in Maimonides' Eschatological Vision," in *Arakhim bi–Mivhan ha–Milhamah* (Alon Shevut: Yeshivat Har Ezion, n.d.), pp. 155–72, note 54 (Hebrew). I cite the translation of Hershman, *Book of Judges*, p. 240.

6. Literally: "and together with Israel will eat permitted foods in tranquillity."

7. XII.1; emphasis added.

8. These are "Laws of Hagigah," III.1 and III.6; "Laws of Gifts to the Poor," X.1; "Laws of Hametz and Matzah," VII.4; and "Laws of Kings," IV.10. My thanks to Rabbi Yehudah Assaf of the Maimonides Research Institute in Haifa for his kindness in procuring references for me from the still unpublished volumes of Rabbi David Assaf, *Ozar Leshon ha–Rambam: Konkordanziah li–Sefer Mishneh Torah*, which is being published by the Maimonides Research Institute.

9. On the Noahide commandments see Steven S. Schwarzschild, "Do Noachites Have to Believe in Revelation?" *JQR* 52 (1962): 297–308 and 53 (1962): 30–65 (reprinted in M. Kellner [ed.], *The Pursuit of the Ideal: Jewish Writings of Steven Schwarzschild* [Albany: SUNY Press, 1990]: 29–59); and David Novak, *The Image of the Non–Jew in Judaism* (New York: Mellen, 1983). For a detailed proof that Maimonides does not mean that today's Gentiles will come under the heading of *ger toshav* in the messianic era (persons who explicitly accept the seven Noahide commandments without fully converting to Judaism) see my article, "A Suggestion," pp. 259–60, and this chapter, pp. 43–45.

10. Hebrew, *goyim*; Hershman has "heathens."

11. XII.4, Hershman, p. 242. On this contrast the view of R. Sa'adia Gaon, *Beliefs and Opinions*, treatise VIII, chapter 6.

12. The passage continues, "Or that it [Israel] might eat and drink and rejoice." Just as the Sages did not look forward to the messianic era because they thought that then Jews would satisfy their carnal desires, so they did not look forward to that time

because they thought that Jews would rule over the gentiles (as did Rav Sa'adia, as we saw).

13. XII.2.

14. Hebrew: *kifi ko'ah ha–adam*; Hershman renders, "to the utmost capacity of the human mind." On this expression see the important study by Aviezer Ravitzky, cited in this chapter, note 3.

15. XII.5; emphasis added.

16. See Shlomo Pines, "The Limitations of Human Knowledge According to Al–Farabi, ibn Bajjah, and Maimonides," in Isadore Twersky (ed.), *Studies in Medieval Jewish History and Literature*, 1 (Cambridge: Harvard University Press, 1979): 82–109; and Altmann, "Maimonides on the Intellect."

17. See Maimonides's commentary to Mishnah Hagigah, II.1; Kafih, II, p. 251.

18. See chapter 4, note 1.

19. See chapter 8.

20. Note here should be taken of "Laws of Idolatry," II.4. "Whoever denies idolatry confesses his faith in the whole Torah, in all the prophets, and all that the prophets *were commanded.*" (I cite the translation of Moses Hyamson, p. 68a; emphasis added). Since the whole world will be full of the knowledge of God, idolatry will be rejected, and *ipso facto* the Torah (including its commandments) will be accepted. In connection with the passage cited in the text here, note should be taken of the distinction I draw below in chapter 9 (p. 82) between *the Jews* and *Israel.*

21. The question of whether or not Maimonides thought that the distinction would disappear because the Gentiles would formally convert need not detain us here. See Blidstein, *Ekronot Mediniim*, pp. 227–34; and my article, "A Suggestion," note 34.

22. XI.4; presented by Hershman on pp. xxiii–xxiv. See Hershman's comments there and Leah Naomi Goldfeld, "Laws of Kings, their Wars, and the King Messiah," *Sinai* 91 (1983): 67–79 (Hebrew).

23. Compare Halevi's parable of the seed in *Kuzari*, IV.23 and Crescas, *Light of the Lord*, II.iv.3 (end). Pines, "Shi'ite Terms," appendix vii (p. 250f) points out the parallel with Halevi; Yizhak Twersky, "Maimonides and the Land of Israel: Halakhic, Philo-

sophic, and Historical Aspects," *Tarbut vi–Hevrah bi–Toldot Yisrael bimei ha–Benaim* (Haim Hillel Ben Sasson Festschrift) (Jerusalem: Merkaz Zalman Shazar, 1989): 353–81, (Hebrew) p. 376n, points out some of the differences between Maimonides and Halevi here.

24. XII.1; see also XI.3. For an example of how the world will follow its normal course after the coming of the Messiah, see Maimonides's comments toward the end of his "Epistle to Yemen" about how the world will find out about the messianic advent. The Messiah will make his first appearance in the land of Israel, and then "the tidings will spread to the East and to the West until it will reach Yemen and those beyond you in India." Apparently, then, news of the Messiah's coming will be spread through normal channels of communication, not through some miraculous, instantaneous process. I quote from the translation of Halkin in *Crisis and Leadership*, p. 125.

25. Maimonides does not specify that he is talking about Christianity, but the reference can be to no other religion.

26. Presumably a statue of Mercury.

27. Translated by Moses Hyamson, Maimonides, *The Book of Adoration* (Jerusalem: Boys Town, 1962), p. 158a (with emendations).

28. See the wonderment expressed in the *Tur*, O. H. 224.

29. This is the third of three explanations offered by R. Joseph Karo; the first is that the Yerushalmi so rules and the second is that R. Simeon b. Elazar is adding to the original position, not contradicting it. His third reason is that *mistaber ta'amei*. This might mean, not that Maimonides agreed with R. Simeon's position, but that R. Simeon's position made sense; that is, that R. Karo also accepted the logical force of R. Simeon's position. This seems unlikely to me: If so, why did R. Karo find the need to justify Maimonides's decision?

30. A third passage in Maimonides's writings also supports our reading of the last chapters of "Laws of Kings." The text, however, may not actually have been written by Maimonides so I cite it here in a note. In a letter to R. Hasdai ha–Levi Maimonides explains why the Sages asserted that the righteous of the Gentile nations of the world have a share in the world to come. They will have a share in the world to come, Maimonides stipulates, "if they have apprehended that which it is proper to apprehend of the knowledge

of the Creator, blessed be He and have improved their souls with virtuous qualities." Maimonides continues, "There is no doubt that everyone who has improved his soul with the propriety of the virtues and with the propriety of wisdom in the faith in the Creator, blessed be He, is certainly among the children of the world to come." (For the text and discussion about it, see Yizhak Shilat [ed. and trans.], *Iggerot ha–Rambam* [Jerusalem: Ma'aliyot, 1987 (vol. 1) and 1988 (2)], 2, p. 673ff. Shilat's hesitancy about ascribing the letter to Maimonides is supported by Jacob S. Levinger, who based himself on the work of Hannah Kasher. See Levinger's *Ha–Rambam ki–Philosoph u–ki–Posek*, pp. 167–71.) The world to come is most certainly not the messianic era according to Maimonides (see "Laws of Repentance," VIII and IX), but the point of the messianic era is to maximize the possibility of achieving the world to come ("Repentance," IX.2) and we have seen that the era of the Messiah will be characterized by the fact that "the one preoccupation of the *whole* world will be to know the Lord."

31. Joel Kraemer, "On Maimonides' Messianic Posture," in I. Twersky (ed.), *Studies in Medieval Jewish History and Literature*, 2 (Cambridge: Harvard University Press, 1984): 109–42, p. 115.

32. I quote from my translation of Isaac Abravanel, *Principles of Faith* (East Brunswick, N.J.: Associated University Presses for the Littman Library of Jewish Civilization, 1982), p. 76.

33. On this, see Lawrence Kaplan, "Maimonides on the Singularity of the Jewish People" *Da'at* 15 (1985): v–xxvii, p. v, citing [and correcting] Y. Leibowitz and W. Z. Harvey.

34. For confirmation that this is Maimonides's position, see his "Laws of Kings," XI.8 and my discussion of that text in chapter 8. Note well Maimonides's comments on Aristotle adduced there.

35. Note that I have added here the word *subordinate*. While it is theoretically possible to affirm that Jew and Gentile in the messianic era will be "separate but equal" (and thereby to reject the reasoning of the US Supreme Court in its 1954 *Brown vs. Board of Education* ruling), in point of fact no premodern Jewish thinker has advanced this view. Those who affirm that Jew and Gentile will retain their distinctive characteristics in the world of the Messiah all affirm that the status of the messianic Gentiles will be inferior to that of the messianic Jews.

36. Yevamot 24b and Avodah Zarah 3b.

37. On this locution, see p. 35.

38. "Laws of Forbidden Intercourse," XIII.15.

39. "Laws of Forbidden Intercourse," XIII.5. It has been argued that Maimonides here means that proselytes who converted before the coming of the Messiah will, once it becomes possible, bring the sacrifices mandated. This is a terribly forced interpretation. We are asked to believe that without any sort of explanation or qualification Maimonides includes here a decision, the scope of which extends only to those individuals converted to Judaism in the years immediately prior to the coming of the Messiah and who survive into the messianic era.

40. See also "Laws of Kings," VIII.10. For some further support of the overall thesis of this chapter, see my discussion in chapter 8 on "Laws of the Sabbatical Year and Jubilee," XIII.13, at p. 74.

41. For details, see Steven Schwarzschild, "A Note on the Nature of Ideal Society."

42. This discussion is drawn from my article, "A Suggestion," p. 260.

43. "Laws of Idolatry," X.17; see also "Laws of Circumcision," I.6; "Laws of the Sabbath," XX.14; "Laws of Forbidden Intercourse," XIV.8; and "Laws of the Sabbatical Year and Jubilee," X.9.

44. "Laws of Kings," XI.1.

45. See Arakhin 29b and Kiddushin 38b.

46. "Laws of Forbidden Intercourse," XIV.7. The reference to "Laws of Idolatry" is to X.6 where Maimonides maintains that when circumstances allow it, Jews are not permitted to suffer idolators in their midst. See also "Laws of the Sabbath," XX.14.

47. "Laws of the Temple," VII.14. The prohibition of granting semiconverts a place in Jerusalem is one of a long list of things prohibited because of the holiness of the city. Given the nature of the list, being placed there is not very complimentary to semiconverts.

48. Compare also "Laws of the Passover Sacrifice," IX.7.

49. "Laws of Kings," XII.1.

50. "Laws of Kings," XI.4.

51. "Laws of the Murderer," II.11.

52. "Laws of the Murderer," II.4.

53. "Laws of Creditor and Debtor," V.1.

54. Ya'akov Blidstein, *Ekronot Medini'im bi–Mishnat ha–Rambam*, pp. 227–34.

55. R. Jacob ben Zvi Emden (1697–1776) entertained the possibility that the *Guide* was not written by Maimonides, the author of the *Mishneh Torah*. See Jacob J. Schachter, "Rabbi Jacob Emden's *'Iggeret Purim*," Isadore Twersky (ed.), *Studies in Medieval Jewish History and Literature*, vol. 2 (Cambridge: Harvard University Press, 1984), pp. 441–46. My thanks to Prof. Sid Z. Leiman for this reference.

Chapter 6

1. Indeed, according to some authorities (Maimonides among them; see note 12) the commandment appears 36 times in the Bible. Thirty–six is a significant number in Jewish reckoning, being twice eighteen, the numerical equivalent of the Hebrew word *hai*, "life." The fact that the commandment was repeated so often may be an indication that its repetition was necessary.

2. See William G. Braude, *Jewish Proselyting in the First Five Centuries of the Common Era—The Age of the Tannaim and Amoraim* (Providence: Brown University Press, 1940).

3. See above, p. 5.

4. Maimonides's letters to Rabbi Obadiah may be found in the edition of Y. Shilat, 1, pp. 231–41, from which they will be quoted (in my translation) here. The Hebrew text of the letters (they were apparently written in Hebrew) is also found in Blau's edition of *Teshuvot ha–Rambam* (Jerusalem: Mekize Nirdamim, 1958), nos. 293, 436, and 448. English translations may be found in Franz Kobler, *Letters of the Jews Through the Ages*, 1 (London: East and West, 1952): 194–97; Solomon B. Freehof, *A Treasury of Responsa* (Philadelphia: Jewish Publication Society, 1962): 28–34 [reprint: New York, Ktav, 1973]; and in Isadore Twersky, *A Maimonides Reader* (New York: Behrman House, 1972): 475–76.

5. It is a likely inference that Rabbi Obadiah was moved to ask the question because there were texts or authorities that held that he should not so pray.

6. Megillah 14a. Note again (compare p. 35 and p. 42n7.), Maimonides's use of "return."

7. Shilat, p. 234. = I. Twersky, pp. 475–76. One wonders if Maimonides means to hint here that Abraham is not "the father of those of his descendants who are *not* proper and *do not* follow in his ways."

8. Halevi's attitude is that proselytes are not fully the equal of native Jews. See chapter 1, note 20; and Daniel J. Lasker's "Proselyte Judaism."

9. Shilat, p. 234 (= Twersky, p. 476).

10. Shilat, p. 235 (= Twersky, p. 476).

11. Shilat, p. 240 (= Twersky, p. 477).

12. That Maimonides was apparently willing to ignore the express command to love one's fellow (Deut. 9:18) in order to emphasize the special nature of the obligation to love the proselyte would only seem to confirm the importance Maimonides seems to attach to convincing his readers to love the proselyte. It is further interesting to note that Maimonides brings up the issue of love of proselytes in contexts where it is wholly unnecessary. Maimonides prefaces his *Book of Commandments* with fourteen discrete discussions about what counts as a commandment. In the ninth of these discussions, casting about for an example of a commandment that is repeated but only counts as one, he cites the rabbinic idea that love of the proselyte is commanded thirty–six times. Plenty of other examples could have been used; he chose this one, I submit, because of his desire to inculcate the idea as deeply as possible in the Jewish mind.

13. Halakhah mandates several differences between native Jews and proselytes, to the disadvantage of the latter. For examples of Maimonides's codification of these see "Laws of Yibbum," IV.5, "Forbidden Intercourse," XIX.12–13, "Sanhedrin," XX.9, XI.11, and "Testimony," XVI.6. It may be that I am wrenching Maimonides's words out of context here and that all he meant to say was that the convert, unlike the semiconvert (with whom the convert is here compared), must obey all the commandments of the Torah.

14. Compare the comments of Yizhak Twersky in his article, "Maimonides and the Land of Israel," p. 380.

15. See my article, " A Suggestion" and my *Dogma in Medieval Jewish Thought*, pp. 19, 226–27. See also below, chapter 8.

16. I write "chooses" advisedly; so far as I can determine, no other codifier included this passage in his codification of the laws of conversion. I have checked the *Halakhot* of Alfasi, the *Tur*, the *Shulhan Arukh*, and the *Arukh ha–Shulhan*.

17. I skip the prooftexts from the Bible. Maimonides's source appears to be a text in Tractate Gerim (II.5). "Just as Israel were initiated into the covenant by three precepts, so proselytes are initiated by circumcision, immersion, and a sacrifice. [The omission of the] first two debars him [from becoming a proselyte], but [the omission of] the third does not debar him." I quote from the text as translated in A. Cohen (ed.), *The Minor Tractates of the Talmud* (London: Soncino Press, 1971), II, pp. 606–7. Maimonides expands on this text by providing the biblical support for the Talmud's claims.

18. Further confirmation of the special character of Maimonides's views here can be had by comparing his codification of the laws of conversion with that of one of his major medieval sources, the *Halakhot* of R. Yizhak Alfasi and with the texts of two of his major successors, the *Arba'ah Turim* and the *Shulhan Arukh* ("Yoreh De'ah" 268). All three of these texts, like Maimonides's, are based on the baraita in Yevamot. But not one of them includes the introductory paragraphs, added by Maimonides, in which native and converted Jews are shown to have become Jewish in the same way, and none of them add the comments found in Maimonides to which attention is drawn in the following paragraph.

19. See the text in chapter 7 at p. 62.

20. "Laws of Forbidden Intercourse," XIV.2; emphasis added.

21. Compare *Mishneh Torah*, "Laws of First Fruits," IV.3 and the interesting discussion of *Mishneh le–Melekh ad loc*.

22. While other decisors follow Maimonides here, he seems to have been the first to decide the law in this fashion.

23. This same passage is given a less welcoming (and less accurate) cast in the translation of A. M. Hershman (p. 230). "Moses, our teacher, bequeathed the Law and commandments to Israel, as it said *an inheritance of the congregation of Jacob* (Deut. 33:4), and to

those of the other nations who are willing to be converted (to Judaism), as it said, *One law and one ordinance shall be for both of you, and for the resident alien* (Num. 15:16)." Here we have people "who are willing to be converted." Maimonides actually spoke of "all those who wish to convert" (*u–li–khol ha–rozeh li–hitgayyer mi–she'ar ha–umot*) a much more positive formulation.

24. Attention must also be drawn to the fact that Maimonides is neither unaware of the *halakhic* disabilities of converts nor does he ignore them in his code. See, for example, the sources cited in note 13. Fully aware of them, and codifying them as he must, he still extends the hand of welcome we have seen.

25. See J. Blau (ed. and trans.), *Teshuvot ha–Rambam* (Jerusalem: Mekize Nirdamim, 1957 [vol. 1], 1960 [vol. 2], 1961 [vol. 3], 1986 [vol. 4, published by Rubin Mass for Mekize Nirdamim]), no. 149 (= vol. 2, p. 284).

26. Perhaps because it is dangerous, either to the faith of the Jew, or in the world in which Maimonides lived, to his or her life? In general, Maimonides's attitude toward Islam (as opposed to Mulims) was much more positive than his attitude toward Christianity, on which see the article by Novak cited in the next note. Perhaps, since Muslims were not in Maimonides's eyes idolaters, while Christians were (see Novak in the next note), it made more sense to proselytize Christians than Muslims: the former need it, so to speak, more than the latter. Note should also be taken of the interesting discussion in Eliezer Schlossberg, "Maimonides' Attitude Toward Islam," *Pe'amim* 42 (1990): 38–60 (Hebrew). Schlossberg argues that Maimonides's personal attitude toward Islam was very negative; it was only in his *halakhic* assessment of its theology that it fared better in his eyes than Christianity.

27, For commentary on this text see Jose Faur, *Iyyunim ba–Mishneh Torah li–ha–Rambam* (Jerusalem: Mossad ha–Rav Kook, 1978), p. 235; Isadore Twersky, *Introduction to the Code of Maimonides* (New Haven: Yale University Press, 1980), p. 414; and, more extensively, David Novak, "The Treatment of Islam and Muslims in the Legal Writings of Maimonides," William Brinner and Stephen Ricks (eds.), *Studies in Islamic and Judaic Traditions* (Atlanta: Scholars Press, 1986): 233–50, p. 244; and Schlossberg (see previous note), pp. 45–46. Note Maimonides's use of the term *return* here in connection with the discussion in chapter 5, p. 35.

28. The question of Jewish attitudes toward proselytization, as

opposed to attitudes toward proselytes themselves, is a complex one. As much as academic accounts of Jewish matters are often colored by the views and institutional affiliations of the academics involved, allegedly historical accounts of Jewish attitudes concerning attempts actively to missionize among the Gentiles seem particularly prone to this problem. For an excellent survey of discussions of the issue that exemplify the problem, see William G. Braude, *Jewish Proselyting in the First Five Centuries of the Common Era*, pp. 3–10. Given the complexities of the situation, all I feel confident in asserting about Maimonides's position is that I am not familiar with other medieval decisors who share his apparently positive attitude toward proselytization.

29. Kiddushin 70b, quoted by Maimonides in "Forbidden Intercourse," XIII.18. For a discussion of the talmudic background and linguistic aspects of Maimonides's comment here, see Shraga Abramson, "Four Discussions on Maimonides," *Sinai* 70 (1972): 24–33 (Hebrew).

30. I skip the prooftexts.

31. "Forbidden Intercourse," XIII.17.

32. By this I mean that since all humans would become Jews in the messianic world, propagandizing in favor of proselytes was a way of preparing Jews for the messianic world, thereby contributing to its realization.

33. I do not mean to imply in what I have written here that Maimonides was trying to do away with received *halakhic* practice (a totally unsupportable hypothesis); nor do I mean to imply that Maimonides was ignorant of the emotional factors involved in the decision to convert; least of all do I mean to imply that identification with the Jewish people is not an important element in conversion for Maimonides (for a reading of Maimonides that emphasizes this last point and resolutely ignores the sorts of issues we have adduced here, see Aharon Lichtenstein, "On Conversion," *Tradition* 23/2 [1988]: 1–18). All of these matters are important, but still secondary to the act of intellectual commitment (on which, see chapter 7).

Chapter 7

1. See my book, *Dogma*, pp. 10–65.

2. I cite the translation from *Dogma*, p.16, where the terms in this passage are explained. For the Arabic source and a Hebrew translation, see Kafih, *Mishnah*, IV, p. 216.

3. This suggestion was first made by Isaac Abravanel in his "Short Treatise Explaining the Secret of the *Guide*," printed at the end of the Vilna, 1864 edition of the *Guide* (and of the many reprints and photo–editions of that edition), and at the end of his "Answers to Shaul ha–Kohen Ashkenazi." Arthur Hyman makes the point again in his "Maimonides' 'Thirteen Principles'," in A. Altmann (ed.), *Jewish Medieval and Renaissance Studies* (Cambridge: Harvard University Press, 1967): 119–44.

4. See "Laws of Moral Qualities," VI.3 for the obligation to love a fellow Jew. In "Laws of the Murderer," XIII.14 Maimonides strongly implies that it is permissable to hate a Jew who does not believe in *ikkar ha–dat* (i.e., the principle of religion), implying, therefore, that such a person has lost the rights that one derives from being a Jew.

5. It is Maimonides's position that the "size" of one's portion in the world to come depends upon the extent to which one has actualized one's intellect, and not on the basis of the care with which one has performed the commandments. One is to obey the commandments without reference to other–worldly reward and, indeed, there is none for such obedience. See "Laws of Repentance," chapter VIII.

6. It must be remembered that it is forbidden to hate a fellow Jew! See "Laws of Moral Qualities," VI.5 and negative commandment 302 in the list of commandments that prefaces the *Mishneh Torah*.

7. Compare "Laws of Idolatry," II.5–6, V.5, and X.6 and *Book of Commandments*, negative commandments 17–21.

8. For a detailed analysis of Maimonides's position here, see my article, "Inadvertent Heresy in Jewish Thought in the Middle Ages: Maimonides and Abravanel vs. Duran and Crescas?" *Jerusalem Studies in Jewish Thought* 3 (1984): 393–403 (Hebrew).

9. Kafih, p. 217.

10. See Isadore Twersky, *Introduction to the Code of Maimonides* (New Haven: Yale University Press, 1980), pp. 474–75.

11. I quote the Soncino translation. Maimonides's text is "Forbidden Intercourse," XIV.2.

12. On this issue, see Gerald Blidstein, "Who Is Not a Jew—The Medieval Discussion," *Israel Law Review* 11 (1976): 369–90.

13. See "Laws of Idolatry," II.5 and X.1; "Repentance," III.7–8; "Tefilin," I.13; "Murderer," IV.10; "Mourning," I.10; "Testimony," XI.10, "Ritual Slaughtering," IV.14 "Robbery," XI.2; "Rebellious Elders," III.2; and *Teshuvot* (ed. J. Blau), #263 (vol. 2, p. 499) and #264 (vol. 2, pp. 499–501) and chapter 9, p. 87. See also my discussion of these texts in my article, "A Suggestion," p. 253 and in my *Dogma,*, pp. 16–21. See also *Guide*, I.36 (p. 85).

14. Whether one sees Maimonides's position as a *substitution* for the received opinion, as I do, or as an *addition* to it, it still needs explanation.

15. See *Dogma,*, pp. 3–7, 18, and 34–49 and my "Inadvertent Heresy."

16. See my article, "A Suggestion."

17. *Tradition and Crisis*, p. 26.

18. Note here should be made of the apparent seriousness of the way in which Maimonides makes the claims that the entire Torah comes to root out idolatry (which, as the parable of the palace in *Guide*, III.51 makes clear, is tantamount to the acceptance of false doctrines about God; this is also the point of Maimonides's refusal to accept the possibility of inadvertence with respect to heresy—for whatever reason it is held, false doctrine excludes one from the community of Israel) and that one who denies idolatry in effect accepts the entire Torah. See *Guide* III.37 (p. 542): "Inasmuch as the intent of the whole Law and the pole around which it revolves, is to put an end to idolatry," and p. 545: "He accordingly would believe things concerning this image to which the whole wish of the Law runs counter, as becomes clear from all the texts of the *Torah*." See further, "Laws of Idolatry," II.4: "Acceptance of idolatry is tantamount to repudiating the whole Torah . . . and whoever denies idolatry confesses his faith in the whole Torah . . . and this is the fundamental principle of all the commandments." The same points are made also in *Guide*, III.29, where we read, "For the foundation of the whole of our Law and the pivot around which it turns, consists in the effacement of these [idolotrous] opinions from the minds and of these [idolotrous] monuments from existence" (p. 521) and that concludes with a citation from *Sifri* to Numbers 15:23 (etc.) to the effect that "everyone who professes

idolatry, disbelieves in the Torah in its entirety; whereas he who disbelieves in idolatry, professes the Torah in its entirety" (p. 522).

19. There is not much he can do about the fact that the *halakhah* considers a person born of a Jewish mother fully Jewish.

Chapter 8

1. For a fascinating modern application of this Maimonidean approach see Steven Schwarzschild, "J.–P. Sartre as Jew," *Modern Judaism* 3 (1983): 39–73, reprinted in M. Kellner (ed.), *The Pursuit of the Ideal*, pp. 161–84. If Isaac Deutscher spoke of the *Non–Jewish Jew*, Schwarzschild, and a certain extent Maimonides, think in terms of the "Jewish non–Jew."

2. As the Gemara *ad loc.* notes, the text is ambiguous and could mean in front of three students or in the presence of three people (the teacher included) altogether.

3. Arabic: *usul.* This term is one of two that Maimonides uses for his "thirteen principles of faith." On this, see my *Dogma*, pp. 17f.

4. See Rabbi Kafih's text. As he notes there, this passage is missing from the standard translations, probably because of homeoleuteton.

5. Arabic: *al–ilm al–ilahi*; the commonly accepted term in medieval Arabic for *metaphysics*. Maimonides, in his *Art of Logic*, XIV explicitly defines "divine science" as "metaphysics" (*ma ba'da al–tabia*). For the Arabic text of *Art of Logic* (*Millot ha–Higayon*) see Israel Efros, "Maimonides' Arabic Treatise on Logic," *PAAJR* 34 (1966): 9–42 (Hebrew section) and 155–60 (English section); the text in question here appears on p. 40. In general, see Harry A. Wolfson, "The Classification of Sciences in Mediaeval Jewish Philosophy," in his *Studies in the History and Philosophy of Religion* I (Cambridge: Harvard University Press, 1973): 493–545.

6. Arabic: *jumlat al–wujud*; probably from the Greek, *ousia*, "being *qua* being," the subject matter of metaphysics for Aristotle. See *Metaphysics*, VI,1, 1026a.

7. Arabic: *al–'ilm al–ilahi.*

8. Quoted from the translation of Israel Efros, *Maimonides'*

Treatise on Logic (New York: American Academy for Jewish Research, 1938), pp. 62–63 with minor emendations. For the study of transcendent ("separate") entities as the subject matter of metaphysics, see Aristotle, *Metaphysics,* VI,1, 1026a.

9. See "Laws of the Foundations of the Torah," II.11.

10. See also "Foundations," II.3 where the angels are called *zurot nifradot zo mi–zo* and the comments of Shlomo Pines on Maimonides's use of the term *zurot* in "God, the *Kavod* and the Angels According to a Twelfth Century Theological System," *Jerusalem Studies in Jewish Thought* 6 (1987): 1–12, p. 11 (Hebrew).

11. Each of these issues involves entities "separate" from matter, that is, transcendent entities.

12. "Laws of the Foundations of the Torah," II.12.

13. Arabic: *al–'ilm al–ilahi; Guide,* I, Introduction (p. 6).

14. Maimonides, along with almost every other ancient and medieval philosophical author, whether Jew, Christian, or Muslim, maintained that the Jews were originally the masters of scientific and philosophical knowledge that they subsequently lost. On this issue see my discussion of *Guide,* II.11 at p. 93, and chapter 3, note 10.

15. See Wolfson, "Classification of the Sciences," pp. 525ff.

16. Compare *Metaphysics,* VII.7 and XII.3.

17. They are also, it should be noted, the two sciences concerning which Maimonides said (in the Hagigah commentary, p. 377), "Because of the importance of these two sciences, the natural and the divine,—*and they were correctly considered important*—we were warned against teaching them like the other preparatory [i.e., mathematical] sciences." (emphasis added).

18. Arabic: *fiqh;* Ibn Tibbon: *Talmud;* Kafih: *dinim.*

19. Arabic: *'ilm as–saria ala l–haqiqa;* Ibn Tibbon: *hokhmat ha–Torah al ha–emet;* Kafih: *yediat ha–Torah bi–emet.*

20. See *Guide,* II. 10 (p. 273) where the *Mishneh Torah* is called "our great compilation on the legalistic study of the Law [*fiqh*]." Compare "Foundations of the Law," IV.13 and p. 38 in Leo Strauss, "The Literary Character of the *Guide of the Perplexed*," in S. W. Baron (ed.), *Essays on Maimonides* (New York: Columbia University Press, 1941): 37–91.

21. This paragraph is based upon pp. 270f. of my essay, "The Conception of Torah as a Deductive Science in Medieval Jewish Thought."

22. For Abravanel's critique of Maimonides and his followers see my "Gersonides and His Cultured Despisers: Arama and Abravanel," *Journal of Medieval and Renaissance Studies* 6 (1976): 269–96; and Alvin Reines, *Maimonides and Abrabanel on Prophecy* (Cincinnati: Hebrew Union College Press, 1970).

23. On this priority, compare "Foundations of the Torah," IV.13.

24. And thus Maimonides calls knowledge "of the forbidden and the permitted and similar things from the rest of the commandments," "a small thing" ("Foundations," IV.13), much to the consternation of commentators like Rabad of Posquières.

25. And thus, in "Laws of the Foundations of the Torah," IV.13 Maimonides tells us that we must first fill our bellies with bread and meat ("knowledge of what is forbidden and permitted") before we approach physics and metaphysics (*ma'aseh bereshit* and *ma'aseh merkavah*).

26. Note well that in "Foundations of the Torah," IV.9 we are informed that the human form, after its separation from the body, "knows and apprehends the intellects separate from body [i.e., the angels], and knows the Creator of all, and [therefore] exists forever and ever." Remember also that, according to *Art of Logic*, knowledge of God and the angels are the preeminent issues in metaphysics.

27. *Guide*, II.40 (p. 384).

28. I quote from the translation of A. S. Halkin in *Crisis and Leadership*, pp. 99–100.

29. The same idea finds expression in the first of Maimonides's major works, the general introduction to his commentary to the Mishnah. See Kafih, *Mishnah*, I, p. 42; and p. 125 in Fred Rosner (trans.), *Moses Maimonides' Commentary on the Mishnah: Introduction to the Mishnah and Commentary on Tractate Berachoth* (New York: Feldheim, 1975).

30. In this connection a valuable insight of David Hartman's ought to be cited.

Maimonides [in his Introduction to *Helek*] appeals to the

Torah, arguing that the Torah itself indicates the existence and legitimacy of universal criteria of truth: *For this is your wisdom and your understanding in the sight of the nations which shall hear all these statutes and say, Surely this great nation is a wise and discerning people* [Deut. 4:6]. If there are specific Jewish criteria of truth, how could this promise be realized? If what counts for truth in this community is to be based exclusively on rabbinic authority, how can the Torah expect those who are not bound by that authority to marvel at and appreciate the wisdom of the community? There must exist, then, independent criteria of truth which neither Jew nor non–Jew can ignore.

I quote from Hartman's *Maimonides: Torah and Philosophic Quest* (Philadelphia: Jewish Publication Society, 1976), pp. 32–33.

31. For studies of these chapters, see Miriam Galston, "The Purpose of the Law According to Maimonides," *Jewish Quarterly Review* 69 (1978): 27–51; and Joel Kraemer, "*Nomos* and *Sharia* in Maimonides' Thought," *Te'udah* (Tel_Aviv University Annual of Jewish Studies) 4 (1986): 185–202 (Hebrew).

32. II.39, p. 378 (emphasis added). Compare "Laws of Idolatry," I.3.

33. II. 39 (p. 381), emphasis added. I have slightly emended the translation to make it more literal. For "all human beings" Pines has "everyone."

34. Arabic: *al–nas kulluhum;* Ibn Tibbon: *bnai adam kulam;* Kafih: *kol bnai adam.*

35. I say "supporting and supported by" because Maimonides saw obedience to the Torah as an almost necessary prerequisite for the apprehension of its philosophical truths and maintained that apprehension of these truths brings one to a higher level of obedience. This interpretation is spelled out and defended in my book, *Maimonides on Human Perfection.*

36. I refer to "Laws of the Sabbatical Year and Jubilee," XIII.13.

37. My attention was drawn to it by Steven Schwarzschild in "Moral Radicalism and 'Middlingness' in the Ethics of Maimonides," in M. Kellner (ed.), *The Pursuit of the Ideal,* p. 317. Actually, there is no significance to these numbers: Maimonides did not

number the specific *halakhot* in the *Mishneh Torah* (see p. iv of Hyamson's introduction to his translation of the *Book of Knowledge*).

38. That is, he is brought to this by his *knowledge*.

39. That is, reverts to the primeval (philosophical) monotheism that Maimonides affirms to have been humanity's native state ("Laws of Idolatry," I.1) and to which Abraham, as we saw, sought to return people through philosophical argumentation.

40. I quote, with emendations, from the translation of Isaac Klein, *The Code of Maimonides Book Seven: The Book of Agriculture* (New Haven: Yale University Press, 1979), p. 403. The significance of the tribe of Levi in this context should not be overlooked. In a number of places Maimonides, building on rabbinic sources, emphasizes the special loyalty to the teachings of the Torah exhibited by this tribe. Note, for example, "Laws of Idolatry," I.2. By comparing Gentiles moved to worship God to Levites, then, Maimonides gives further evidence of his positive attitude toward them.

41. On the worship of God as philosophical meditation, see *Guide*, III.51, M. Fox, "Prayer in the Thought of Maimonides," in G. Cohen (ed.), *Ha–Tefilah ha–Yehudit: Hemshekh vi–Hiddush* (Ramat Gan: Bar Ilan University Press, 1978): 142–67 (Hebrew), and my book, *Maimonides on Human Perfection*, pp. 31–33.

42. See chapter 6, p. 54.

43. The text here can be seen as an explanation of Maimonides's previous uses of the term in the *Mishneh Torah:* "Laws of Repentance," III.5, "Forbidden Intercourse," XIV.7, and "Testimony," XI.10.

44. *Hekhra ha–da'at.*

45. I quote from the translation of A. M. Hershman, p. 230, with emendations.

46. For a handy survey of the textual, historical, hermeneutical, and historical questions and writings based on our text, see Jacob I. Dienstag, "Natural Law in Maimonidean Thought and Scholarship (On *Mishneh Torah*, Kings, VIII.11)," *Jewish Law Annual* 6 (1987): 64–77. The fate of bibliographers is brought out by the fact that essays in the same and subsequent volume of the *Jewish Law Annual* render Dienstag's fine survey incomplete.

47. It is taken up, however, in the letter to R. Hasdai ha–Levi attributed to Maimonides and cited in chapter 5, note 30. There

are many, however, who doubt this attribution, and so I do not want to rely upon this text here. The text in question reads as follows:

> With respect to what you asked concerning the nations [of the world]: Know that God requires the heart, and everything depends upon the heart's intention. Thus, the true Sages, our Rabbis, peace upon them, said that "the righteous gentiles have a place in the world to come," [Tosefta Sanhedrin, XIII] if they have apprehended that which it is proper to apprehend of the knowledge of the Creator, blessed be He and improved their souls with virtuous qualities. There is no doubt that everyone who has improved his soul with the propriety of the virtues and with the propriety of wisdom, in the faith in the Creator, blessed be He, is certainly among the children of the world to come. Thus the true Sages, our Rabbis, peace upon them, said, "If one is a gentile, but studies [lit.: deals with] the Torah, he is like the High Priest" [Bava Kama 38a].

There is no mention here that the righteous Gentile must accept the Noahide commandments *because* they are commanded in the Torah.

    There is an English translation of this letter in Leon D. Stitskin, *Letters of Maimonides* (New York: Yeshiva University Press, 1977): 95–112.

    Reverting to the text under discussion here, as I read it, Maimonides explains in the opening sentence that righteous Gentiles have a portion in the world to come. The closing sentence distinguishes wise Gentiles from righteous ones without determining whether or not they have a portion in the world to come. Indeed, on his own doctrine of immortality (see my book, *Maimonides on Human Perfection*, chapter 1 and above, pp. 10–15) Maimonides could not restrict it to righteous Gentiles; intellectual perfection is the key to immortality, nothing else.

    48. See "Laws of Forbidden Intercourse," XIV.7:

> What is meant by a "resident alien"? A former heathen who has undertaken to forsake the worship of idols and to observe the other commandments made obligatory upon the descendants of Noah, but has been neither circumcised nor immersed. He should be accepted and regarded as one

of the "righteous gentiles." Why is he called "resident"? Because we are allowed to permit him to reside in our midst in the Land of Israel [as opposed to idolators, who must be expelled from the land].

I quote here with emendations from the translation of Louis I. Rabinowitz and Philip Grossman, *The Book of Holiness* (New Haven: Yale University Press, 1965), p. 93.

49. Hebrew (the Arabic original of the letter is lost): *da'ato*. Another possible translation is "his knowledge." On Maimonides's use of this term, see David Baneth, "Maimonides' Philosophical Terminology," *Tarbiz* 6 (1935): 258–84 (Hebrew), p. 260; and David R. Blumenthal, "Maimonides on Mind and Metaphoric Language," in D. R. Blumenthal (ed.), *Approaches to Judaism in Medieval Times* II (Chico, Calif.: Scholars Press, 1985): 123–32.

50. The inconsistency between singular and plural is in the text, but less grating to the ear in Hebrew (especially medieval Hebrew) than in English.

51. I quote from the edition of Shilat, vol. 2, p. 553. On this letter see Alexander Marx, "Texts By and About Maimonides," *JQR* 25 (1934–35): 374–81; Alfred Ivry, "Islamic and Greek Influences on Maimonides' Philosophy," S. Pines and Y. Yovel (eds.), *Maimonides and Philosophy* (Dordrecht: Martinus Nijhoff, 1986): 139–56; and Shlomo Pines, "Translator's Introduction," p. lix, in Pines's translation of the *Guide*.

52. See also II. 23 (p. 332). Jose Faur plays down the significance of these passages, interpreting them so as to diminish Maimonides's admiration for Aristotle. See his *Iyyunim ba–Mishneh Torah li–ha–Rambam*, p. 7. I find Faur's interpretation forced, an estimation reinforced by the fact that Shem Tov ibn Falaquera, Maimonides's great thirteenth–century admirer, criticized the Master for his excessive admiration of Aristotle. See Henry Malter, "Shem Tob ben Joseph Palquera II: His 'Treatise of the Dream'," *JQR* 1 (1910–11): 451–501, p. 492.

53. Shilat, vol. 2, p. 481.

Chapter 9

1. This comes out very clearly in many places. In his "Epistle to Yemen," for example, he speaks of the preeminence of the Jew

(Halkin translation, pp. 96–97) and of the "pure and undefiled lineage of Jacob" (p. 103); see also "Laws of Repentance," II.10.

2. Studies of Maimonides's attitude toward the Jewish people include Yaakov Levinger, "Prophecy among the Gentiles According to Maimonides," *Ha–Ma'ayan* 12 (1971): 16–22 (Hebrew); Levinger, "The Uniqueness of Israel, Its Land, and Its Language according to Maimonides," *Mil'et* (Open University Studies in Jewish History and Culture), 2 (Tel Aviv: Open University, 1984): 289–97 (Hebrew); Haim Hillel Ben–Sasson, "The Uniqueness of Israel According to Twelfth Century Thinkers," *P'raqim* (Schocken Institute Yearbook), 2 (1969–74): 145–218 (Hebrew) (pp. 165–96 on Maimonides); Dov Rappel, "The Status of the Nations and Their Purpose in the Teachings of R. Judah Halevi and Maimonides," in *Mishnato he–Hagutit shel R. Yehudah Halevi* (Jerusalem: Ministry of Education and Culture, 1978): 119–22 (Hebrew), and Lawrence Kaplan, "Maimonides on the Singularity of the Jewish People." I have seen a reference to, but have not read, G. Chernowitz, *Ha–Yahas bein Yisrael la–Goyyim lifi ha–Rambam* (New York, 1950).

3. *Exodus Rabbah*, XLVII.3, translated by S. M. Lehrman (London: Soncino, 1939), p. 538.

4. *Sifra* to Lev. 16:16. This passage serves as the motto for Michael Wyschogrod's *The Body of Faith: Judaism as Corporeal Election* (New York: Seabury Press, 1983). Wyschogrod argues for a consciously and explicitly anti–Maimonidean reading of the nature of the Jewish people, insisting on a notion of election explicitly based on God's choice of the Jews as a people. This, he admits, is hard to understand. "This is the crux of the mystery of Israel's election. Seen through the eyes of man, a divine election of a group defined by some ideological criterion would seem far more plausible" (p. 57). As I will demonstrate in this chapter, the position that Wyschogrod rejects here is precisely that of Maimonides (that, of course, does not mean that Wyschogrod is wrong, although he is). For Maimonides, as I argued in chapter 5, in the days of the Messiah all human beings will constitute the elect.

5. That is, if they neglect it. Maimonides's decision here concerning the descendents of Keturah is a minority one. Most decisors maintain that there is no obligation to circumcize them. See *Enzyklopediah Talmudit*, III (Jerusalem: Talmudic Encyclopedia Publications, 1951), p. 382.

6. Compare Isadore Twersky's more muted formulation of this point: "Maimonides' spiritual conception of Judaism, in which biological factors are rather insignificant," in his *Introduction to the Code of Maimonides* (New Haven: Yale University Press, 1980), p. 486.

7. See chapter 6, p. 50.

8. I cite from Hyamson's translation, p. 66b, with emendations. It appears that Maimonides here combines aggadot with the sort of philosophical tale his slightly older contemporary Ibn Tufayl developed in his "Hayy ibn Yaqzan." See Louis Ginzberg, *Legends of the Jews*, 1 (Philadelphia: Jewish Publication Society, 1968), pp. 195–98; and Lenn Evan Goodman, *Ibn Tufayl's Hayy ibn Yaqzan* (Los Angeles: Gee Tee Bee, 1983).

9. Abraham, that is, came to knowledge of God through philosophic conviction, not religious faith. On this distinction, see my "The Virtue of Faith," in Lenn Evan Goodman (ed.), *Judaism and Neoplatonism* (Albany: SUNY Press, in press).

10. Hyamson, pp. 66b–77a, with emendations and emphasis added.

11. *Guide* I.63 (pp. 153–54).

12. In the continuation of the text quoted from "Idolatry," I.2, Maimonides makes it clear that Isaac and Jacob were as motivated by philosophical considerations as was Abraham.

13. *Guide*, II.39, p. 379.

14. "Laws of Forbidden Intercourse," XIII.1; see the discussion in chapter 6, p. 52.

15. See chapter 7, p. 62.

16. Compare Halevi, *Kuzari*, I.87: "The people prepared and became fitted to receive the divine afflatus, and even to hear publicly the words of God . . . they distinctly heard the Ten Commandments . . . from God . . . the people saw the divine writing, as they had heard the divine words" (pp. 60–61).

17. Makkot 24a.

18. Precisely the principles of faith that Maimonides says must be taught to the prospective convert. "He should then be made acquainted with the principles of the faith, which are the oneness

of God and the prohibition of idolatry. These matters should be discussed in great detail" ("Forbidden Intercourse," XIV.2).

19. That is, proved.

20. Commentary to Mishnah Sanhedrin, X.3; see chapter 7, p. 63.

21. See chapter 7, p. 62.

22. For more details, see my article, "A Suggestion Concerning Maimonides' Thirteen Principles," pp. 251–53. Further on the need and obligation to kill heretics, see "Epistle to Yemen," Halkin translation, p. 114.

23. In my *Dogma in Medieval Jewish Thought*, pp. 42ff. I show how the first five of Maimonides's thirteen principles, which in his eyes are rationally demonstrable (actually, the first four are, while the fifth, not to worship any entity but God, is a consequence of them) are in his eyes the most important and crucial of the thirteen.

Our discussion to this point allows us to solve a puzzle. There are two areas in which Maimonides does not apply his strictures against the heretic, etcetera: with respect to marriage and the taking of interest. Why does he not inform us that a marriage entered into by a heretic is invalid (compare "Laws of Forbidden Intercourse," XIII.17 and "Laws of Marital Relations," IV.15) and why does he not inform us that we may take interest from a heretic? The reason, I submit is as follows: the heretic, sectarian, and *epikoros* have excluded themselves from the community of Israel, but that does not change the brute biological fact that they are Jews by birth. Marriage restrictions are first and foremost a matter of lineage; we are forbidden to take interest from our *brother* (Lev. 25:35–37; Deut. 23:20–21); Maimonides was thus unable to impose his strictures on theological deviants in these two cases and did not.

24. "Epistle to Yemen," Halkin translation, p. 96. On this point, compare Sa'adia's well-known dictum, "Our nation is only a nation by virtue of its laws" (*Beliefs and Opinions*, III.7).

25. P. 97; emphasis added.

26. P. 108. On Maimonides's general lack of attention to the notion of the chosen people, see *Encyclopaedia Judaica* (Jerusalem: Keter, 1971), 5, col. 501.

27. P. 114; emphasis added. The Arabic for "religious community" is *milla*, which means exactly that, as opposed to *ummah*, or nation. To the best of my knowledge there is no study of Maimonides's use of the term. For its use in Al–Farabi see p. 151 in Joel Kraemer, "Alfarabi's *Opinions of the Virtuous City* and Maimonides's *Foundations of the Law*," in J. Blau, *et al.* (eds.) *Studia Orientalia: Memoriae D. H. Baneth Dedicata* (Jerusalem: Magnes, 1979): 107–53; George Vajda, "Language, philosophie, politique et religion, d'apres un traite recemment publie d'Abu Nasr al–Farabi," *Journal Asiatique* 257 (1970): 240–60, p. 256; and the following studies by the late Lawrence V. Berman: "A Re–Examination of Maimonides' Statement on Political Science," *Journal of the American Oriental Society* 89 (1969): 106–111, p. 108; "Maimonides, the Disciple of Al–Farabi," *Israel Oriental Studies* 4 (1974): 154–78, p. 165; and (with I. Alon) "Socrates on Law and Philosophy," *Jerusalem Studies in Arabic and Islam* 2 (1980): 263–79, p. 264.

28. See Abravanel's analysis in *Rosh Amanah*, chapter 10. In my translation, *Principles of Faith*, pp. 98–195.

29. Rabbi Joseph Kafih, *Ha–Mikra bi–Rambam* (Jerusalem: Mossad ha–Rav Kook, 1972).

30. "To give charity" is an alternative translation for the words translated as "to do righteousness" in 18:19.

31. "Laws of Forbidden Intercourse," XIX.17 might be cited as a counterexample, since Maimonides there asserts that Jews are by nature merciful. In "Laws of Slavery," IX.8, however, he explains that Jews are merciful because the Torah has educated them to be merciful. My attention was drawn to these passages by Levinger, *Ha–Rambam*, p. 89.

32. Arabic: *milla*.

33. Shilat, vol. 1, p. 234.

34. Compare Maimonides further commentary to this verse cited by his son (and quoted by Levinger, *Ha–Rambam*, p. 89) which begins, "Through the observance of my Torah you will become leaders of the world." See further Maimonides's explanation of why a Jew must help a sinful Jew whose animal has collapsed under its load: "he might delay in order not to lose money and thus become endangered. The Torah is very careful of the lives of Israelites, whether wicked or righteous, *since they accompany God and*

believe in the principle of religion" (emphasis added) ("Laws of the Murderer" 13:14). The Torah is solicitous of the wellbeing of Israelites because of their adherence to proper belief, not because of their Abrahamic descent.

35. Arabic: *milla*. Pines translates "community," offering "nation" as an alternative. Since Maimonides immediately cites Deut. 4:6, where the term *am* (nation, people) appears, we have further evidence for our thesis: Maimonides in effect here translates the Hebrew *am* (nation, people) into the Arabic *milla* (religious community).

36. Hebrew: *am*. Pines renders this as "community" an odd translation of the Hebrew, and obviously influenced by Maimonides's use of the Arabic *milla*.

37. Compare Marvin Fox, "Law and Morality," Nahum Rakover, *Maimonides as Codifier of Jewish Law* (Jerusalem: Library of Jewish Law, 1987): 105–20, pp. 112 and 119 on Jews who render themselves so base as to be barely human.

38. In a different context, Eliezer Goldman, "Political and Legal Philosophy in the *Guide for the Perplexed*," in Nahum Rakover (ed.), *Maimonides as Codifier of Jewish Law* (Jerusalem: Library of Jewish Law, 1987): 155–64, presents what can be construed as an alternative explanation for the impossibility of Maimonides's having adopted an essentialist reading of the nature of the Jewish people: "Human nature is regarded by Maimonides as both uniform and constant. The uniformity follows from the Aristotelian conception of the 'nature' of a species. Human nature is what it is to be human. Differences between individuals cannot be accounted for by differences in their natures. Were they to differ in nature, only one of them could be human. The constancy follows from the Aristotelian notion of the eternity of natural species" (pp. 155–56).

39. An astute and anonymous reader of this book has raised an interesting objection to the thesis defended in this chapter in particular and in the book in general. Why could not Maimonides maintain, in light of the climatological theories widely accepted in his day, that while the Jews are not metaphysically distinct from Gentiles, the fact that they originate from the most perfect part of the world makes them better predisposed than others to receive the Torah? This is a way of sneaking an essentialist reading of the nature of the Jewish people into Maimonides's thought through the back door. For information on climatological theories in the

ancient and medieval world, and for an analysis of Halevi's use of them, see Alexander Altmann, "The Climatological Factor in Yehudah Hallevi's Theory of Prophecy," *Melilah* 1 (1944): 1–17. Now, despite the fact that Maimonides does indeed (like most scientists of his day) accept a version of the climatological theory (see, e.g., *Iggerot ha–Rambam*, ed. and trans. Rav J. Kafih [Jerusalem: Mossad ha–Rav Kook, 1972], pp. 149–50), he nowhere in fact uses this theory to defend the special character of the Jews or assert that they have a greater predisposition toward intellectual excellence and thus a head start over other peoples in terms of being ready to receive the Torah. For a valuable discussion of this issue and convincing argument to the effect that not only did Maimonides not adopt the sort of view against which I argue in this note, but that he *could not* have adopted such a view, see Abraham Melamed, "The Land of Israel and the Climatological Theory in Medieval and Renaissance Jewish Thought," *Erez Yisrael ba–Mahshavah ha–Yehudit* (Jerusalem: Yad Ben Zvi, in press) (Hebrew).

Conclusion

1. It might be objected that I have no proof that Maimonides's psychology preceded his religious positions. Perhaps his religious positions came first and he adopted his psychology because of them. This is most unlikely. What I have called Maimonides's religious positions are unusual while his psychology was prevalent in philosophical circles in his day. It strains credulity to suppose that the religious positions came first, therefore, and that the psychological theory was adopted because of them.

2. Note the argument in *Dogma,* pp. 42ff. to the effect that it was the first five principles, all of which deal with doctrines concerning God (i.e., with metaphysics = *ma'aseh merkavah*), which truly concerned Maimonides.

3. To my mind, that congruity is so central to his thought that it is illegitimate to speak of "philosophical" as opposed to "religious" positions in Maimonides. They are all the same. The "foundation of all [religious] foundations" is identical with the "pillar of the [philosophical] sciences" ("Laws of the Foundations of the Torah," I.1). (For the source of this interpretation see Isaac Abravanel, *Rosh Amanah,* chapter 5; in my translation, p. 76.)

4. See Frederick M. Denny's remarkably fine *Introduction to Islam* (New York: Macmillan, 1985), p. 145.

5. See Lawrence V. Berman, "Maimonides, the Disciple of Al-farabi," *Israel Oriental Studies* 4 (1974): 154–78; and the discussion of Berman's position in my book, *Maimonides on Human Perfection*, pp. 49–53.

6. Pines's usage; see his "Translator's Introduction," p. cxvii and chapter 1, p. 6.

7. Yizhak Twersky, "On Law and Ethics in the *Mishneh Torah*: A Case Study of *Hilkhot Megillah*, II:17," *Tradition* 24 (1989): 138–49, pp. 139–40.

Works Cited

Abramson, Shraga. "Four Discussions on Maimonides," *Sinai* 70 (1972): 24–33 (Hebrew).

Abravanel, Isaac. *Commentary on the Guide of the Perplexed.*

———. *Commentary on the Torah.*

———. *Crown of the Elders* (Warsaw, 1894).

———. *Principles of Faith* (East Brunswick, N.J.: Associated University Presses for the Littman Library of Jewish Civilization, 1982), translated by Menachem Kellner.

———. "Short Treatise Explaining the Secret of the *Guide*."

Alfasi, Yizhak. *Halakhot.*

Altmann, Alexander. "Maimonides on the Intellect and the Scope of Metaphysics," in Altmann's *Von der mittelalterlichen zur modernen Aufklaerung* (Tuebingen: Mohr, 1987): 60–129.

———. "The Climatological Factor in Yehudah Hallevi's Theory of Prophecy," *Melilah* 1 (1944): 1–17 (Hebrew).

Assaf, David. *Ozar Leshon ha–Rambam: Konkordanziah li–Sefer Mishneh Torah* (Haifa: Maimonides Research Institute, n.d.).

Baneth, David. "Maimonides' Philosophical Terminology," *Tarbiz* 6 (1935): 258–84 (Hebrew).

Ben–Sasson, Haim Hillel. "The Uniqueness of Israel According to Twelfth Century Thinkers," *P'raqim* (Schocken Institute Yearbook) 2 (1969–74): 145–218 (Hebrew).

151

Berman, Lawrence V. "A Re–Examination of Maimonides' Statement on Political Science," *JAOS* 89 (1969): 106–11.

————. "Maimonides, the Disciple of Alfarabi," *Israel Oriental Studies* 4 (1974): 154–78.

————. (with I. Alon). "Socrates on Law and Philosophy," *Jerusalem Studies in Arabic and Islam* 2 (1980): 263–79.

————. "Some Remarks on the Arabic Text of Maimonides' 'Treatise on the Art of Logic'," *JAOS* 88 (1968): 340–42.

Bibago, Abraham. *Path of Faith* (Constantinople, 1522; photoreproduction, Jerusalem: Mekorot, 1970).

Bleich, J. David. *Providence in the Philosophy of Gersonides* (New York: Yeshiva University Press, 1973).

Blidstein, Gerald (Ya'akov). "Who Is Not a Jew—The Medieval Discussion," *Israel Law Review* 11 (1976): 369–90.

————. *Ekronot Medini'im bi–Mishnat ha–Rambam* (Ramat Gan, Israel, Bar Ilan University Press, 1983).

————. "On Universal Rule in Maimonides' Eschatological Vision," in *Arakhim bi–Mivhan ha–Milhamah* (Alon Shevut: Yeshivat Har Ezion, n.d.): 155–72 (Hebrew).

Blumenthal, David R. "Maimonides on Mind and Metaphoric Language," in Blumenthal (ed.), *Approaches to Judaism in Medieval Times*, II (Chico: Scholars Press, 1985): 123–32.

Braude, William G. *Jewish Proselytizing in the First Five Centuries of the Common Era—The Age of the Tannaim and the Amoraim* (Providence: Brown University Press, 1940).

Buijs, Joseph. "The Philosophical Character of Maimonides' *Guide*— A Critique of Strauss' Interpretation," *Judaism* 27 (1978): 448–57.

Chernowitz, G. *Ha–Yahas bein Yisrael la–Goyyim lifi ha–Rambam* (New York, 1950).

Cohen, A. (ed.) *The Minor Tractates of the Talmud* (London: Soncino Press, 1971).

Crescas, Hasdai. *Light of the Lord* (Vienna, 1859).

Davidson, Herbert A. "Alfarabi and Avicenna on the Active Intellect," *Viator* 3 (1972): 109–78.

———. "Maimonides' *Shemonah Peraqim* and Alfarabi's *Fusul al–Madani*," *PAAJR* 31 (1963): 33–50.

———. "Sa'adia's List of Theories of the Soul," in A. Altmann (ed.), *Jewish Medieval and Renaissance Studies* (Cambridge: Harvard University Press, 1967): 75–94.

———. "The Middle Way in Maimonides' Ethics," *PAAJR* 54 (1987): 31–72.

———. *The Philosophy of Abraham Shalom* (Berkeley: University of California Press, 1964).

Denny, Frederick M. *Introduction to Islam* (New York: Macmillan Publishing Co., 1985).

Dienstag, Jacob I. "Natural Law in Maimonidean Thought and Scholarship (On *Mishneh Torah*, Kings, VIII.11)," *Jewish Law Annual* 6 (1987): 64–77.

Diesendruck, Zvi. "Samuel and Moses ibn Tibbon on Maimonides' Theory of Providence," *HUCA* 11 (1936): 341–66.

Efros, Israel. "Maimonides' Treatise on Logic: The New Arabic Text and Its Light on the Hebrew Versions," *JQR* 53 (1962–63): 267–73.

Enzyklopediah Talmudit, III (Jerusalem: Talmudic Encyclopedia Publications, 1951).

Even–Shmuel, Yehudah. *Midrashei Ge'ulah* (Tel Aviv: Mossad Bialik/Massada, 1943).

Exodus Rabbah. Translated by S. M. Lehrman (London: Soncino, 1939).

Fakhry, Majid. "The Contemplative Ideal in Islamic Philosophy: Aristotle and Avicenna," *Journal of the History of Philosophy* 14 (1976): 137–45.

Faur, Jose. *Iyyunim ba–Mishneh Torah li–ha–Rambam* (Jerusalem: Mossad ha–Rav Kook, 1978).

Feldman, Seymour. "Gersonides on the Possibility of Conjunction with the Agent Intellect," *AJS Review* 3 (1978): 99–120.

Fox, Marvin. "Law and Morality," in Nahum Rakover (ed.), *Maimonides as Codifier of Jewish Law* (Jerusalem: Library of Jewish Law, 1987): 105–20.

———. "Prayer in the Thought of Maimonides," in G. Cohen (ed.), *Ha–Tefilah ha–Yehudit: Hemshekh vi–Hiddush* (Ramat Gan, Israel, Bar Ilan University Press, 1978): 142–67 (Hebrew).

———. "The Doctrine of the Mean in Aristotle and Maimonides: A Comparative Study," in S. Stein and R. Loewe (eds.), *Studies in Jewish Religious and Intellectual History Presented to Alexander Altmann* (University [Alabama]: University of Alabama Press, 1987): 93–120.

Frank, Daniel H. "Humility as a Virtue: A Maimonidean Critique of Aristotle's Ethics," in Eric L. Ormsby (ed.), *Moses Maimonides and His Time* (Washington: Catholic University of America Press, 1989): 89–99 (= *Studies in Philosophy and the History of Philosophy*, 19).

Freehof, Solomon B. *A Treasury of Responsa* (Philadelphia: Jewish Publication Society, 1962; reprint: New York, Ktav, 1973).

Funkenstein, Amos. "Maimonides: Political Theory and Realistic Messianism," *Miscellanea Mediaevalia* 9 (1977): 81–103.

———. *Teva, Historiah, u–Meshihiut ezel ha–Rambam* (Tel Aviv: Ministry of Defense, 1983).

Galston, Miriam. "The Purpose of the Law According to Maimonides," *Jewish Quarterly Review* 69 (1978): 27–51.

Ginzberg, Louis. *Legends of the Jews*, 1 (Philadelphia: Jewish Publication Society, 1968).

Goldfeld, Leah Naomi. "Laws of Kings, Their Wars, and the King Messiah," *Sinai* 91 (1983): 67–79 (Hebrew).

Goldman, Eliezer. "Political and Legal Philosophy in the *Guide for the Perplexed*," in Nahum Rakover (ed.), *Maimonides as Codifier of Jewish Law* (Jerusalem: Library of Jewish Law, 1987): 155–64.

Goodman, Lenn Evan. *Ibn Tufayl's Hayy ibn Yaqzan* (Los Angeles: Gee Tee Bee, 1983).

Greenstone, Julius. *The Messiah Idea in Jewish History* (Philadelphia: Jewish Publication Society, 1906).

Guthrie, W. K. C. "Plato's Views on the Nature of the Soul," *Entretiens sur l'antiquite classique,* 3: *Recherches sur la tradition Platonicienne* (Geneva: Vandoeuvres, 1955): 3–19.

Hallamish, Moshe. "Some Aspects of the Attitudes of the Kabbalists Towards Gentiles," in Asa Kasher and Moshe Hallamish (eds.), *Philosophiah Yisraelit* (Tel Aviv: Papyrus [University of Tel Aviv]: 1983): 49–71 (Hebrew).

Hartman, David. "Discussion" of Maimonides's 'Epistle to Yemen', in *Crisis and Leadership: Epistles of Maimonides* (Philadelphia: Jewish Publication Society, 1985), translated by A. S. Halkin, discussions by David Hartman: 150–207.

————. *Maimonides: Torah and Philosophic Quest* (Philadelphia: Jewish Publication Society, 1976).

————. "Sinai and Messianism," in Hartman, *Joy and Responsibility* (Jerusalem: Posner, 1983): 232–58.

Harvey, Warren Zev. "Hasdai Crescas' Critique of the Theory of the Acquired Intellect," Ph.D. diss., Columbia University, 1973.

————. "R. Hasdai Crescas and His Critique of Philosophic Happiness." *Proceedings of the Sixth World Congress of Jewish Studies* 3 (Jerusalem: World Congress of Jewish Studies, 1977): 143–49 (Hebrew).

Hertzberg, Arthur. *The Jews in America* (New York: Simon & Schuster, 1989).

Hyman, Arthur. "Aristotle's Theory of the Intellect and Its Interpretation by Averroes," in Dominic J. O'Meara (ed.), *Studies in Aristotle* (Washington: Catholic University of American Press, 1981): 161–91 (= *Studies in Philosophy and the History of Philosophy* 9).

————. "Interpreting Maimonides," *Gesher* 5 (1976): 46–59.

————. "Maimonides' 'Thirteen Principles'," in A. Altmann (ed.), *Jewish Medieval and Renaissance Studies* (Cambridge: Harvard University Press, 1967): 119–44.

Ibn Daud, Abraham. *The Exalted Faith by Abraham ibn Daud* (Rutherford, N.J.: Farleigh Dickinson University Press and London: Associated University Presses, 1986), edited by Gershon Weiss and translated by Norbert M. Samuelson.

Ivry, Alfred. "Islamic and Greek Influences on Maimonides' Philosophy," in S. Pines and Y. Yovel (eds.), *Maimonides and Philosophy* (Dordrecht: Martinus Nijhoff, 1986): 139–56.

Jacob ben Asher. *Arba'ah Turim.*

Judah Halevi, *Kuzari* (New York: Schocken Books, 1964), translated by Hartwig Hirschfeld.

Kafih, Joseph. *Ha–Mikra bi–Rambam* (Jerusalem: Mossad ha–Rav Kook, 1972).

Kaplan, Lawrence. "Maimonides on the Singularity of the Jewish People," *Da'at* 15 (1985): v–xxvii.

Karo, Joseph. *Shulhan Arukh.*

Katz, Jacob. *Tradition and Crisis: Jewish Society at the End of the Middle Ages* (New York: Schocken Books, 1971).

Kellner, Menachem. "A Suggestion Concerning Maimonides 'Thirteen Principles' and the Status of Non–Jews in the Messianic Era," in Meir Ayali (ed.), *Tura—Oranim Studies in Jewish Thought: Simon Greenberg Jubilee Volume* (Tel Aviv: Ha–Kibbutz ha–Meuhad, 1986): 249–60 (Hebrew).

———. *Dogma in Medieval Jewish Thought* (Oxford: Oxford University Press, 1986).

———. "Gersonides, Providence, and the Rabbinic Tradition," *JAAR* 42 (1974): 673–85.

———. "Inadvertent Heresy in Medieval Jewish Thought: Maimonides and Abravanel vs. Duran and Crescas?" *Jerusalem Studies in Jewish Thought* 3 (1984): 393–403 (Hebrew).

———. *Maimonides on Human Perfection* (Atlanta: Scholars Press, 1990).

———. "Messianic Postures in Israel Today," *Modern Judaism* 6 (1986): 197–209.

———. "The Conception of Torah as a Deductive Science in Medieval Jewish Thought," *REJ* 146 (1987): 265–79.

———. "The Virtue of Faith," in Lenn Evan Goodman (ed.), *Judaism and Neoplatonism* (Albany: SUNY Press, in press).

Klausner, Joseph. *The Messianic Idea in Israel* (New York: Macmillan, 1955).

Kobler, Franz. *Letters of the Jews Through the Ages* (London: East and West, 1952).

Kogan, Barry. "'What Can We Know and When Can We Know it?' Maimonides on the Active Intelligence and Human Cognition," Eric L. Ormsby (ed.), *Moses Maimonides and His Time* (= *Studies in Philosophy and the History of Philosophy* 19) (Washington: Catholic University of America Press, 1989): 121–37.

Kraemer, Joel. "Alfarabi's *Opinions of the Virtuous City* and Maimonides' *Foundations of the Law*," in J. Blau, *et al.* (eds.) *Studia Orientalia: Memoriae D. H. Baneth Dedicata* (Jerusalem: Magnes, 1979): 107–53.

———. "*Nomos* and *Sharia* in Maimonides' Thought," *Teudah* (Tel Aviv University Annual of Jewish Studies) 4 (1986): 185–202 (Hebrew).

———. "On Maimonides' Messianic Posture," in I. Twersky (ed.), *Studies in Medieval Jewish History and Literature*, vol. 2 (Cambridge: Harvard University Press, 1984): 109–42.

Kreisel, Howard. "Maimonides on the Practical Intellect," *HUCA* 69 (1988): 189–215.

Lasker, Daniel J. "Original Sin and its Atonement According to Hasdai Crescas," *Da'at* 20 (1988): 127–35 (Hebrew).

———. "Proselyte Judaism, Christianity, and Islam in the Thought of Judah Halevi," *JQR* 81 (1990) forthcoming.

Lazaroff, Allan. *The Theology of Abraham Bibago* (University: University of Alabama Press, 1981).

Leaman, Oliver. *Moses Maimonides* (London: Routledge, 1990).

Levi ben Gershom (Gersonides), *Wars of the Lord* (Philadelphia: Jewish Publication Society, 1984 [vol. 1], and 1987 [vol. 2]), translated by Seymour Feldman.

Levinger, Ya'akov. *Ha–Rambam ki–Philosoph u–ki–Posek* (Jerusalem: Mossad Bialik, 1989).

———. "Human Perfection among the Gentiles According to Maimonides," *Hagut* II: *Bein Yisrael li–Amim* (Jerusalem: Ministry of Education and Culture, 1978): 27–36 (Hebrew).

———. "Prophecy among the Gentiles According to Maimonides," *Ha–Ma'ayan* 12 (1971): 16–22 (Hebrew).

158   *Works Cited*

———. "The Uniqueness of Israel, Its Land, and Its Language according to Maimonides," in *Mil'et* (Open University Studies in Jewish History and Culture) 2 (Tel Aviv: Open University, 1984): 289–97 (Hebrew).

Lichtenstein, Aharon. "On Conversion," *Tradition* 23/2 (1988): 1–18.

Maimonides. *Book of Adoration* (Jerusalem: Boys Town, 1962), edited and translated by Moses Hyamson.

———. *Book of Agriculture* (New Haven: Yale University Press, 1979), translated by Isaac Klein.

———. *Book of Commandments.*

———. *Book of Holiness* (New Haven: Yale University Press, 1965), translated by Louis I. Rabinowitz and Philip Grossman.

———. *Book of Judges* (New Haven: Yale University Press, 1949), translated by A. M. Hershman.

———. *Book of Knowledge* (New York: Feldheim, 1974), edited and translated by Moses Hyamson.

———. *Commentary on the Mishnah: Introduction to the Mishnah and Commentary on Tractate Berachoth* (New York: Feldheim, 1975), translated by Fred Rosner.

———. "Epistle to Yemen," in *Crisis and Leadership: Epistles of Maimonides* (Philadelphia: Jewish Publication Society, 1985), translated by A. S. Halkin.

———. "Epistle to Yemen," in *Moses Maimonides' Epistle to Yemen* (New York: American Academy for Jewish Research, 1952), edited by A. S. Halkin.

———. *Ethical Writings of Maimonides* (New York: Dover, 1983), edited and translated by R. L. Weiss and C. Butterworth.

———. *Guide of the Perplexed* (Chicago: University of Chicago Press, 1963), translated by Shlomo Pines.

———. *Iggerot ha–Rambam* (Jerusalem: Ma'aliyot, 1988), edited and translated by Ya'akov Shilat.

———. *Iggerot ha–Rambam* (Jerusalem: Mossad ha–Rav Kook, 1972), edited and translated by Joseph Kafih.

——. *Letters of Maimonides* (New York: Yeshiva University Press, 1977), translated by Leon D. Stitskin.

——. "Maimonides' Arabic Treatise on Logic," *PAAJR* 34 (1966): 155–60 (English) and 9–42 (Hebrew), edited by Israel Efros.

——. *Maimonides' Treatise on Logic* (New York: American Academy for Jewish Research, 1938) = *Proceedings of the American Academy for Jewish Research* 10 (1938).

——. *Mishnah im Perush Rabbenu Moshe ben Maimon* (Jerusalem: Mossad ha–Rav Kook, 1963), translated by Joseph Kafih.

Malter, Henry. "Shem Tob ben Joseph Palquera II: His 'Treatise of the Dream'," *JQR* 1 (1910–11): 451–501.

Marx, Alexander. "Texts by and about Maimonides," *JQR* 25 (1934–35): 374–428.

Melamed, Abraham. "The Land of Israel and the Climatological Theory in Medieval and Renaissance Jewish Thought," *Erez Yisrael ba–Mahshavah ha–Yehudit* (Jerusalem: Yad Ben Zvi, forthcoming) (Hebrew).

Montefiore, C. G. and H. Loewe, *A Rabbinic Anthology* (New York: Schocken, 1974).

Novak, David. *The Image of the Non–Jew in Judaism* (New York: Mellen, 1983).

——. "The Treatment of Islam and Muslims in the Legal Writings of Maimonides," William Brinner and Stephen Ricks (eds.), *Studies in Islamic and Judaic Traditions* (Atlanta: Scholars Press, 1986): 233–50.

Nuriel, Avraham. "Providence and Guidance in the *Guide of the Perplexed*," *Tarbiz* 49 (1980): 346–55 (Hebrew).

Pines, Shlomo. Foreward to David Hartman, *Maimonides: Torah and Philosophic Quest* (Philadelphia: Jewish Publication Society, 1976).

——. "God, the *Kavod* and the Angels according to a Twelfth Century Theological System," *Jerusalem Studies in Jewish Thought* 6 (1987): 1–12, p. 11 (Hebrew).

——. "Shi'ite Terms and Conceptions in Judah Halevi's *Kuzari*," *Jerusalem Studies in Arabic and Islam* 2 (1980): 165–251.

———. "The Limitations of Human Knowledge according to Al–Farabi, ibn Bajjah, and Maimonides," in Isadore Twersky (ed.), *Studies in Medieval Jewish History and Literature*, 1 (Cambridge: Harvard University Press, 1979): 82–109.

———. Translator's Introduction, in Maimonides's *Guide of the Perplexed* (Chicago: University of Chicago Press, 1963), translated by Shlomo Pines.

Rahman, Fazlur. *Avicenna's Psychology* (London: Geoffrey Cumberlege for Oxford University Press, 1952).

Rappel, Dov. "The Status of the Nations and Their Purpose in the Teachings of R. Judah Halevi and Maimonides," in *Mishnato he–Hagutit shel R. Yehudah Halevi* (Jerusalem: Ministry of Education and Culture, 1978): 119–22 (Hebrew).

———. "Profiat Duran's Introduction to *Sefer Ma'aseh Efod*," Yizhak Raphael (ed.), *Sinai Centenary Volume* (Jerusalem: Mossad ha–Rav Kook, 1987), Vol. II: 749–795 (Hebrew).

Ravitzky, Aviezer. "According to Human Capacity—The Messianic Era in the Teaching of Maimonides," in Z. Baras (ed.), *Meshihiut vi–Eschatalogiah* (Jerusalem: Merkaz Shazar, 1983): 191–220 (Hebrew).

———. "'The Feet of the Kabbalists Stand Upon the Heads of the Philosophers'?—On the Disputation in Candia in the Fifteenth Century," *Tarbiz* 58 (1990): 453–82.

Reines, Alvin. *Maimonides and Abrabanel on Prophecy* (Cincinnati: Hebrew Union College Press, 1970).

Sa'adia Gaon, *Book of Beliefs and Opinions* (New Haven: Yale University Press, 1948), translated by Samuel Rosenblatt.

Samuelson, Norbert M. "Ibn Daud's Conception of Prophecy, *Journal of the American Academy of Religion* 45 (1977) (Supplement): 883–900.

Sarachek, Joseph. *The Doctrine of the Messiah in Medieval Jewish Literature* (New York: Hermon Press, 1968).

Schachter, Jacob J. "Rabbi Jacob Emden's *Iggeret Purim*," in Isadore Twersky (ed.), *Studies in Medieval Jewish History and Literature*, 2 (Cambridge: Harvard University Press, 1984): 441–46.

Schlossberg, Eliezer. "Maimonides's Attitude Toward Islam," *Pe'amim* 42 (1990): 38–60 (Hebrew).

Scholem, Gershom. *Major Trends in Jewish Mysticism* (New York: Schocken Books, 1941).

————. "Towards an Understanding of the Messianic Idea in Judaism," in *The Messianic Idea in Judaism* (New York: Schocken, 1971): 1–36.

Schwarzschild, Steven S. "A Note on the Nature of Ideal Society—A Rabbinic Study," in Strauss and Reissner (eds.), *Jubilee Volume Dedicated to Curt C. Silberman* (New York: Association of Jews from Central Europe, 1969): 86–15; reprinted in M. Kellner (ed.), *The Pursuit of the Ideal: Jewish Writings of Steven Schwarzschild* (Albany: SUNY Press, 1990): 99–108.

————. "Do Noachites Have to Believe in Revelation?" *JQR* 52 (1962): 297–308 and 53 (1962): 30–65; reprinted in M. Kellner (ed.), *The Pursuit of the Ideal: Jewish Writings of Steven Schwarzschild* (Albany: SUNY Press, 1990): 29–59.

————. "J.-P. Sartre as Jew," *Modern Judaism* 3 (1983): 39–73; reprinted in M. Kellner (ed.), *The Pursuit of the Ideal: Jewish Writings of Steven Schwarzschild* (Albany: SUNY Press, 1990): 161–84.

————. "Moral Radicalism and 'Middlingness' in the Ethics of Maimonides," *Studies in Medieval Culture* 11 (1978): 65–94; reprinted in M. Kellner (ed.), *The Pursuit of the Ideal: Jewish Writings of Steven Schwarzschild* (Albany: SUNY Press, 1990): 137–60.

Shalom, Abraham. *Abode of Peace* (Venice, 1575; photoreproduction; Westmead [England]: Gregg International, 1969).

Silberman, Lou H. "Chosen People," *Encyclopaedia Judaica* (Jerusalem: Keter, 1971), 5, cols. 498–502.

Silman, Yohanan. *Bein Philosoph li–Navi* (Ramat Gan, Israel, Bar Ilan University Press, 1985).

————. "The Systematic Reasons for the Idea of the Election of Israel in the *Kuzari*," *Sinai* 80 (1977): 253–64 (Hebrew).

Silver, Abba Hillel. *A History of Messianic Speculation in Israel* (New York: Macmillan, 1927).

Strauss, Leo. "The Literary Character of the *Guide of the Perplexed*," in S. W. Baron (ed.), *Essays on Maimonides* (New York: Columbia University Press, 1941): 37–91.

————. "Maimonides' Statement on Political Science," *PAAJR* 22 (1953): 115–30.

Tishbi, Isaiah. *Mishnat ha–Zohar* I, 3d. ed. (Jerusalem: Mossad Bialik, 1971).

Tosefta Sanhedrin.

Twersky, Isadore (Yizhak). *A Maimonides Reader* (New York: Behrman House, 1972).

————. *Introduction to the Code of Maimonides* (New Haven: Yale University Press, 1980).

————. "Maimonides and the Land of Israel: Halakhic, Philosophic, and Historical Aspects," *Tarbut vi–Hevrah bi–Toldot Yisrael bimei ha–Benaim* (Haim Hillel Ben Sasson Festschrift) (Jerusalem: Merkaz Zalman Shazar, 1989): 353–81 (Hebrew).

————. "On Law and Ethics in the *Mishneh Torah*: A Case Study of *Hilkhot Megillah*, II:17," *Tradition* 24 (1989): 138–49.

Urbach, Ephraim E. *Hazal* (Jerusalem: Magnes, 1969).

Vajda, George. "Language, philosophie, politique et religion, d'apres un traite recemment publie d'Abu Nasr al–Farabi," *Journal Asiatique* 257 (1970): 240–60.

Weiss, Raymond L. "Law and Ethics: Reflections on Maimonides 'Ethics'," *Journal of the History of Philosophy* 9 (1971): 425–33.

————. "On the Scope of Maimonides' *Logic*, Or, What Joseph Knew," in R. Link–Salinger (ed.), *A Straight Path: Studies in Medieval Philosophy and Culture, Essays in Honor of Arthur Hyman* (Washington, D.C.: Catholic University of America Press, 1988): 255–65.

————. "The Adaptation of Philosophic Ethics to a Religious Community: Maimonides' *Eight Chapters*," *PAAJR* 54 (1987): 261–87.

Wijnhoven, Jochanan H. A. "The Zohar and the Proselyte," in Michael A. Fishbane and Paul R. Flohr (eds.), *Texts and Responses: Studies Presented to Nahum N. Glatzer . . .* (Leiden: Brill, 1975): 120–40.

Wolfson, Harry A. "Hallevi and Maimonides on Prophecy," *JQR* 32 (1942): 345–70 and 33 (1942): 49–82, reprinted in Wolfson, *Studies in the History of Philosophy and Religion*, II (Cambridge: Harvard University Press, 1977): 60–119.

————. "The Classification of Sciences in Mediaeval Jewish Philosophy," in his *Studies in the History and Philosophy of Religion* I (Cambridge: Harvard University Press, 1973): 493–545.

Wyschogrod, Michael. *The Body of Faith: Judaism as Corporeal Election* (New York: Seabury Press, 1983).

Index